Hidden Among Us

The Lives of Contemporary Holy Men and Women of Egypt

VOLUME 1

*The Lives of Fr. Abdel Massih of Manahra,
the Fool for Christ,
and Metropolitan Mena, His Disciple*

ANTHONY MARCOS

Hidden Among Us: The Lives of Contemporary Holy Men and Women of Egypt

Volume 1: The Lives of Fr. Abdel Massih of Manahra, the Fool for Christ, and Metropolitan Mena, His Disciple

By Anthony Marcos

Designed & Published by:
St. Mary & St. Moses Abbey Press
101 S Vista Dr, Sandia, TX 78383
stmabbeypress.com

Cover design by St. Mary & St. Moses Abbey Press

Contents

Preface

If one pauses long enough to consider the state of the world today, they will feel an unmistakable ache in the heart. We are besieged by an absence of peace. We are encircled on all sides by a mounting indifference to God. What was once called virtue is now scorned; what was once clearly immoral is now celebrated.

By simply taking a brief moment to look around, we cannot help but notice the unrest among nations, the division within families, and the subtle, but steady, erosion of all that is holy. Even the very desire to remain in stillness is often not satisfied; we are overwhelmed with commotion, interruption, and disorientation. Faith is treated as utterly obsolete, truth is seen as absolutely relative, and holiness is regarded as completely unrealistic.

The faithful groan. We find ourselves echoing the sighs of the disciples, and reiterating their same troubled question, "Who then can be saved?"[1]

And yet, the apostle Paul responds to our growing anxieties: "where sin abound[s], grace abound[s] much more."[2]

These words of St. Paul are not meant to be poetic; the grace of Christ does not diminish as time advances, nor does

---

1   Mt 19:25.

2   Rom 5:20.

it deteriorate with modernity—heaven forbid! The reality is that the darkness that appears to thicken around us actually becomes the very backdrop with which Christ our God, the True Light, shines even more brightly. The things that feel heavy to the soul can never restrain His light; they can, and they will, only reveal Him more.

It is not a small thing to pursue holiness in a time that makes little room for it. When choosing, for example, to fast when comfort is abundant, or to pray when distraction is constant, or to forgive when "cancel culture" is rampant—this is precisely when the Holy Spirit works! This is when He fashions saints out of average people, people living silently in our midst.

Within these very pages are the stories of "average people."

Some were clergy; others were laypeople. They were ordinary people in ordinary circumstances, though their times, places, and callings may have differed from one another. Yet the common thread among them was this: they lived their lives largely unseen. They remained hidden in the monotonous pace of cities and villages. If you were to find them in their homes or parishes, in the desert, and in the world, you might not recognize them for who they truly were. These people lived quietly. They moved about unnoticed. As you read about them, you may not know many of their names.

They were so hidden that the overwhelming majority of stories and biographies included have never been released previously in English; some, even, have never been written down at all. Much of what is preserved here would have remained known only to a small circle of spiritual children until they, too, departed this life. Had they not been gathered, these accounts may have very well been lost to time (though always be remembered by God).

The story of their lives, as presented here, was derived with the utmost care and integrity from varied primary sources: firsthand written records, oral testimonies, manuscripts, and recorded memoirs of personal disciples. The lives herein have been arranged by leveraging a narrative format to allow the text to be more readable and coherent; slight, inconsequential literary devices and liberties were taken so this writing would flow smoothly, especially where the original accounts were brief, scattered, or preserved only in fragments.

Footnotes and references have been included wherever possible, both to clarify the context of each life and to allow the reader to trace each and every story back to its original, verifiable source. Even so, it is inevitable that some will wish to scrutinize the historical reliability of every detail, or to approach these accounts with a mind focused only on what can be reasoned through and explained logically.

Suffice it to say, the stories you will read here are true.

They are corroborated by witnesses to their veracity. The signs and wonders entailed are substantiated. They are untainted, unexaggerated, unembellished, and, most importantly, a testament to the reality that the Lord Jesus Christ remains active in our fallen world.

These lives have been gathered to affirm that the Holy Spirit continues to raise up saints within the Orthodox Church, and most especially, within the Coptic Orthodox Church of Alexandria. On that note, I cannot help but write this plainly and without apology: there are those who challenge her, who willfully mischaracterize her, and even deny that she continues to produce saints, as in centuries past. The stream of sanctity that flowed through the desert fathers and the martyrs of the Coptic Orthodox Church has not dried up, not for a moment; and these biographies are written as an indication of that undeniable fact.

Furthermore, historicity alone is not the reason these lives were compiled. We did not decide to dedicate ourselves to writing these accounts because of a mere academic interest, nor did we do this to simply produce a catalogue of a few supernatural events.

The conviction arose from something far more urgent: the need to bear witness.

We must bear witness to the grace of God, which remains vigorous in our own lifetime. We need to convey that, even in an age of gross spiritual decline, the Lord has not withdrawn His hand. That holy hand still takes, blesses, sanctifies, and distributes to nourish the entire world. The world, for all its darkness, is not barren of holiness. To say that the world is void of saints is to say that Christ has ceased from working in His creation.

These accounts are intended to awaken, to stir the heart. They serve as a reminder that the call to holiness is not reserved for another century. The saints were not born different from us. They struggled, repented, fell, rose again, and pressed forward. What distinguished them was their refusal to live divided; they realized that they could not bear to live half-attached or half-surrendered.

And when a man completely surrenders himself to God, the work of God in him begins, but it is often concealed for a season. Yet for the edification of His Holy Church, the Lord does not leave His children hidden under a basket; at the appointed hour, He lifts them out of obscurity and sets them upon a lampstand, that through them, He may dispel the darkness of the world.

We must trust that He is able to make saints, even out of us. We must not—actually, we cannot—lose hope, even when our sins seem many, and our weaknesses are persistent.

After all, His grace abounds exceedingly more than our sin ever could.

The apostle writes, "For this is the will of God, your sanctification."[3]

Hence, His will is for us to become saints. And the greatest tragedy in life is leaving the earth having not become one.

May these pages draw you closer to the Holy Trinity. May they encourage your repentance. May they deepen your prayer. May they kindle a longing for the life of holiness that is offered freely to every believer, including you. And may the blessing of these righteous ones remind you that sanctity is not far away.

Sanctity is nearer than we think.

Sanctity is within arm's reach, in our midst.

Sanctity is hidden among us.

---

3   1 Thess 4:3.

The Life of Fr. Abdel Massih of Manahra
The Fool for Christ

Introduction

Fr. Abdel Massih of the Monastery of St. Macarius,[4] also known as Abdel Massih of Manahra,[5] is widely regarded as one of the greatest, albeit unsung, contemporary saintly men to come from the Church of Alexandria. Though he is now widely venerated, Fr. Abdel Massih largely lived in obscurity. He was rarely noticed, and even more rarely understood. Only those closest to him could see through his careful, intentional efforts to conceal his virtues, and yet, many times, even they found themselves uncertain about him, to the point of putting his sanity into question.

Nevertheless, those who approached him with a discerning heart realized that not only was he of sound and sober mind, contrary to what many assumed, but that he, unquestionably, was nothing short of a spiritual giant.

He lived in a time not far removed from our own, and yet this blessed monastic often drew comparisons to the elders of early Christian monasticism. An instance from the memories of Fr. Raphael Abba Mena, who served as a disciple

---

4   Al-Maqari (المقاري) refers to his association with the Monastery of St. Macarius the Great.

5   Al-Manahri (المناهري) denotes his connection to the village of Manahra, a small village located in the Governorate of Beni Suef, approximately 200 kilometers (124 miles) south of Cairo. There, Fr. Abdel Massih served for over three decades, and eventually lived as a recluse until his repose.

to St. Pope Kyrillos VI, illustrates the spiritual stature of this contemporary desert father.

Fr. Raphael evokes to memory:

I never met Fr. Abdel Massih, since he departed in 1963; however, whenever those who visited [Pope Kyrillos] came from Manahra, or Minya, or Beni Suef [where Fr. Abdel Massih served], His Holiness would ask them, "Is Fr. Abdel Massih still alive, my son?"

They would reply, "Yes, Your Holiness."

His Holiness would respond and say, "Abba Macarius is still alive then, my son." I thought this was because Fr. Abdel Massih was from the Monastery of St. Macarius.

As the days passed, another came from Manahra, and he would ask, "How is Fr. Abdel Massih, my son? Is he still alive?"

He answered, "He's alive and well, Your Holiness."

"How wonderful! Abba Paul [the First Hermit] is alive, my son!"

Days passed, and he would ask, "Is Fr. Abdel Massih alive, my son?"

"Yes, Your Holiness!"

"Abba Anthony is alive then, my son!"

Once he called him, "Abba Macarius," and the second time he called him, "Abba Anthony," and the third time he called him, "Abba Paul." What is all of this? All of these in one individual?

CHAPTER ONE

Birth, Upbringing, and Monastic Tonsure

In the village of Abu Shehata, in the district of Matai, a wealthy livestock owner named Henein looked down into his arms and gazed upon the face of his firstborn, whom he named Samaan. He would be the only son in the family, an older brother to seven sisters. The entire family legacy would be entrusted to his care.

The exact date of his birth is unknown for certain, although Metropolitan Mena of Girga (1919–2003), the disciple and biographer of Fr. Abdel Massih of the Monastery of St. Macarius, writes:[6]

> With great effort did I attempt to find the exact date of his birth, but I was unable to…. I found a note in his own handwriting on the inside cover of his personal *Euchologion* [The Book of the Three Divine Liturgies], now in the possession of one of his loved ones; it records the year of his tonsure as a monk, "1914 AD–1630 AM".… If we take into

---

6   Metropolitan Mena of Girga, *Seerit Qidees Mo'aser: Al-Qis Abdel Massih Al-Maqari* [The Life of a Contemporary Saint: Fr. Abdel Massih of the Monastery of St. Macarius]. (Egypt: 1979), 15–16. [Henceforth, The Arabic Life of Fr. Abdel Massih.]

consideration that the saint was tonsured at the age of twenty-two, we can deduce he was born in 1892.

Samaan grew and learned his father's trade, tending to the livestock owned by the family, which included sheep, cows, and camels. Samaan was never enrolled in formal education, nor did he attend a single lesson at the village's *kuttab*;[7] he was completely illiterate. He taught himself, with great challenge, to read and write as an adult, immediately prior to his joining the monastery.

And though it took substantial effort to read even a single passage from the Scriptures, it seemed that the more Samaan exposed himself to the word of God, the more it began to work within the depths of his heart. He began to long for solitude, the sweetness of which he tasted while shepherding his father's sheep. And finally, with his frequent retreats to the Monastery of St. Samuel[8] and his constant encounters with the elders therein, the seed of monasticism began to sprout.

---

7   *Kuttab* typically refers to a traditional elementary or primary school in Arabic-speaking countries. In a kuttab, children usually learn the basics of reading, writing, and grammar. Historically, kuttab schools have been fundamental in providing basic education, particularly in rural areas.

8   Located on Mount Qalamun, approximately 60 kilometers (about 37 miles) west of the city of Minya in Upper Egypt, the monastery was founded by Abba Samuel the Confessor (597–695 AD). While living in the Monastery of St. Macarius, Abba Samuel found that an imperial envoy was sent to persuade the desert fathers to accept the Tome of Leo. Burning with zeal, Abba Samuel stood up, took the letter from the envoy's hand, and tore it to pieces. The envoy, enraged, ordered his soldiers to suspend Samuel by his arms and beat him with iron rods. His face was struck with such violence that one of the blows caused the loss of his eye. He was exiled to Mount Qalamun, where others gathered around him, and a monastic community took root; the monastic life is still active there to this day. He is commemorated on the 8th day of the Coptic month of Koiahk, coinciding with December 17, having reposed at the good old age of 98.

Samaan managed to persuade his father to grant him permission to observe Holy Week at the monastery, despite knowing he was expected back for work immediately after the Feast of the Resurrection. However, upon the agreed day of his return, Samaan did not return.

His father waited, one day after the other, left to tend to the flock on his own. He never returned. Finally, Henein's frustration reached its limit, and he would not allow this to continue.

Henein travelled swiftly to the village of Zawra, then onward to the Monastery of St. Samuel. He insisted on retrieving his wayward son. When he found Samaan sitting in his own designated cell, wrath overtook him. He seized him and quite literally dragged him outside, compelling him to abandon the monastery.

But despite the stern reprimands of his father, and the tearful pleas of his mother Esther and his seven sisters to stay with them, Samaan remained obstinate. His resolve to seek his salvation at St. Samuel's Monastery remained unshaken, and so he attempted to escape to the monastery several times. However, with each escape, his father went to the monastery, brought him back, and thwarted his plans.

In a surprising turn of events, with each forced return home, a mysterious and ominous occurrence befell the family: a significant portion of Henein's livestock inexplicably fell down dead the moment Samaan set foot inside the home. The divine intervention seemed obvious; it was an unmistakable sign urging Samaan's family to let their son enter the monastic life.

Nevertheless, Henein remained unmoved by these obvious heavenly warnings. He hardened his heart and closed his eyes to God's clear interventions. He was determined, instead, to dissuade his son from the path he chose, and so, he decided to do the unthinkable.

One day, Samaan returned home from the farm after a long day of caring for the family's dwindling herd. Exhaustion weighed heavily upon him. His back ached. His hands and feet cramped. He could not wait to throw himself onto his bed.

Yet, as he approached the house, an eerie silence greeted him. There was an unsettling absence of the usual bustle and chatter of women that filled the air—his mother and sisters were all gone. The house had been emptied; Samaan had no idea that his father had sent them all to his uncle's home for the night.

Entering his room at long last, Samaan found a woman lying on his bed.

He was bewildered, furious. Who was she? Why was she in his room?

But before Samaan could get any answers from her, Henein aggressively pushed him into the room and locked the door from the outside. Samaan was now trapped.

A harrowing realization promptly came over him. She was hired by his father.

Henein had offered the woman a substantial sum, and she would only receive it if she succeeded in convincing Samaan to sin with her. He was confident that this wicked strategy would change his son's mind regarding monasticism. He now would have no choice but to get married and live with him. How would he choose celibacy after that night?

This evil woman tried with Samaan just as Potiphar's wife tried with Joseph. Her efforts were futile. Nevertheless, she was adamant about getting the money promised to her. And so, she seized him and attempted to force herself on him.

Samaan shouted in her face, "Get away from me! May there be pain in your stomach!"

As the last word escaped Samaan's lips, she immediately fell to the ground and began writhing on the floor. She grabbed at her stomach and shrieked in agony, "Fire! Coals of fire burning in my stomach!"

Henein, hearing the woman's screams, barged into his son's room, looking on in terror.

"Please," she begged. She crawled on the floor and clutched desperately at the fringe of Henein's tunic, "have your son forgive me! Leave him do what he wants! Shame on you!"

The woman was on the verge of death from her pain. Henein implored his son to forgive her, and Samaan finally uttered a single word, pardoning her. The woman stood up at once, completely healed, and hurried out of the house.

Metropolitan Mena explains what ensued:

Finally, after many attempts to persuade him [to stay with them], his father told him, "My boy, you are my only son! I have no other male children besides you! Would you abandon me and your mother and your sisters?"

The saint told his father, "If the Lord gives you another boy instead of me, would you leave me to go to the monastery?"

His father agreed to that condition.[9]

---

9   The Arabic Life of Fr. Abdel Massih, 17.

With his father's agreement, Samaan offered a hopeful gaze to heaven, and presented a silent plea for the Lord's final divine intervention. Henein and his wife, both well into old age, bore a son. They named him Hanna.

The promise was upheld, and Henein allowed his son to pursue the monastic life. Samaan instantly left for the Wilderness of Scetis,[10] to the Monastery of St. Macarius.

For the 22-year-old, the act of donning a simple black tunic the day of his tonsure merely marked a visible manifestation of his long-enduring way of life. Truly, being a servant to Christ the Messiah had been ingrained in Samaan's very essence, long before he ever set foot on the grounds of the Monastery of St. Macarius. Though it was in the year 1914 that he officially assumed the name Abdel Massih, the truth was that he had always been *Abdel Massih*—"a servant of the Messiah." Shortly after his tonsure, he was ordained a priest.

---

10   The Wilderness of Scetis, known also as the Valley of Natron, or in Arabic, *Wādī al-Naṭrūn*, is a historic region in Egypt's Western Desert, located approximately 100 kilometers (about 60 miles) northwest of Cairo. It is renowned as one of the most significant centers of early Christian monasticism, dating back to the fourth century AD. The area consists of several ancient monastic communities, many of which still thrive to this day.

CHAPTER TWO

Asceticism and Discipleship

The interior life of Fr. Abdel Massih remained shrouded in mystery to his contemporaries. He lived a life of stillness and serenity, regularly seen with a spiritual book under his arm whenever he was seen outside his cell. He often secluded himself within his cell for extended periods, even for weeks at a time, emerging only in cases of dire necessity. No one truly knew what happened within his cell. The only thing that became obvious was that the vast majority of his time inside his cell was devoted entirely to prayer.

One of the unique characteristics of Fr. Abdel Massih was his approach to the monastic principle of discipleship. He approached it with seriousness and drew inspiration not only from the desert fathers of early monasticism, but also from more recent fathers. Under guidance and instruction, he incorporated their methods of ascesis[11] into his own spiritual practices. One such method involved suspending a rope from the ceiling of his cell, which he would secure around his chest

---

11   Ascesis (from the Greek ἄσκησις meaning "exercise" or "training") refers to the spiritual and bodily discipline undertaken to purify the heart and grow in union with God. It encompasses practices such as fasting, prayer, vigils, silence, and obedience, not as ends in themselves, but as means to combat the passions and cultivate virtue. Ascesis is understood not as self-denial for its own sake, but as a synergistic cooperation with divine grace, motivated by love for Christ.

beneath his arms. This practice, reminiscent of the ascetic struggle of Abba Pishoy,[12] served the purpose of preventing him from falling to the floor should he succumb to sleep.

Additionally, he exhibited ingenuity by repurposing the wooden frame of a large sifter, commonly used in the monastery for straining flour. He would tie a rope on opposite ends of the sifter's circular frame, suspend it from the ceiling, and fit himself through it. He then positioned it beneath his arms. This ensured that, should he begin to nod off, and so move in one way or another, the sifter would tug at him under his arms, and instantly rouse him.

Fr. Abdel Massih would maintain this state of vigilance for up to three days at a time. He followed the example of the late Fr. Tadros of the Monastery of St. Macarius, a contemporary of his who was delegated to serve in Syria and later reposed there. As a newly tonsured monk, Fr. Abdel Massih had the opportunity to encounter Fr. Tadros and learn of his ascetic practices.

It was said of Fr. Tadros that he would stand motionless and in prayer for three days and nights, with his hands crossed over his chest. Clergy from the surrounding churches in Syria often stumbled upon him in church, seeing his rigid, motionless posture. They immediately supposed that Fr. Tadros had died

---

12   Abba Pishoy of Scetis (320–417 AD) was an Egyptian desert father. Having joined the monastic life at the age of 20, Pishoy's life of prayer and pursuit of virtue attracted hundreds of disciples to the Wilderness of Scetis. His asceticism was austere, to the extent of tying his hair with a rope to the ceiling of his cell, in order to resist nodding off during his night prayers. Pishoy's hagiography details several personal encounters with the Lord Jesus Christ, who promised him that his body would remain incorrupt after his repose. He is venerated by the Oriental Orthodox Church and the Eastern Orthodox Church, known in the latter under the Greek variant of his name, Paisios. His feast day is celebrated annually on the 8th of Coptic month of Epep, coinciding with July 15.

while standing, and panic took hold of them. But when they realized the truth, they would approach him quietly and kiss his hands as they lay over his chest. They came to understand that his immobility was a manifestation of spiritual ecstasy; in this transcendent state, he was absorbed in holy visions, dissociating completely from his surroundings.

In consensus among all the monastery's fathers, Fr. Abdel Massih had committed the entire Book of the Psalmody[13] to memory, along with the majority of the Church hymns. His voice, though quiet and shy, possessed an unmistakable angelic quality.

Regarding his spiritual rule of fasting, he adopted a rather discreet approach when eating. He would wait until his fellow monks finished their meals at the monastery's refectory. Ensuring no one would witness what he was about to do, Fr. Abdel Massih waited until the dining room was empty. He would approach the table, gather the crumbs of bread scattered about, dip them in water, and dine. Any stray pieces of cooked legumes or vegetables found on the table also became part of his meal.

Following this ritual, he would then abstain from food until the following sunset, eating only once daily. Later in life, the people who would host him explained that he *pretended* to eat early in the morning, so as to avoid appearing to be fasting for extended periods.

---

13   The Psalmody is the Coptic Orthodox Church's book of hymns and praises said throughout the day in Vespers, Midnight, and Matins. It combines biblical odes, psalms, songs to the Lord Jesus Christ, and daily praises to the Blessed Virgin Mary known as *Tadakia* (from the Greek *Theotokia*). Monastic communities developed the Psalmody as a way of maintaining vigil throughout the night, a practice witnessed by John Cassian and other early monastic figures in their travels to Egypt. Today, the Psalmody is not restricted only to monks, as many of the lay-people passionately pray it in their respective parishes and homes.

Discipleship under the elders is paramount for anyone seeking the life of virtue. It was said of Abba Anthony the Great that he frequented the ascetics, one by one, to become acquainted with the virtue each of them excelled in, searching them out as a wise bee searches for sweet-smelling flowers.[14] Fr. Abdel Massih took up residence in the other monasteries of Scetis in search of elders who would disciple him. He found for himself two brothers in the nearby Monastery of Baramous,[15] Fr. Abdel Massih Salib al-Masudi[16] and Fr. Yacoub al-Masudi. The latter became known as "the silent monk" because of a vow of silence he took.

The former of the two, after Fr. Abdel Massih's ordination, allowed him to pursue the solitary life in the desert. Fr. Abdel Massih's feet took him to Jerusalem, and from there, he settled

---

14   "And if he heard about someone who was serious about following good practices, he would go and search out that person like the wise honeybee and would not return to his own place until he had seen that person." St. Athanasius the Apostolic, *The Life of Antony: The Coptic Life and The Greek Life*, Vivian T. and Athanassakis A., trans. (Kalamazoo, MI: Liturgical Press, 2003), 60.

15   Also known as the Monastery of the Romans, it is located in Wadi al-Natrun and was founded in the fourth century by St. Macarius the Great. The name "Baramous" is derived from the Coptic "*Pa-Romeos*," meaning, "of the Romans," signifying its historical connection to the saintly Roman monks Maximus and Dometius, traditionally held as the sons of Emperor Valentinian I, disciples of Macarius, who abandoned their imperial life and resided there. The monastic life flourishes in the Monastery of Baramous to this very day.

16   *Fr. Abdel Massih Ṣalib al-Masudi* (1848–1935), a monk from the Monastery of Baramous, was a prolific Coptic scholar known for his writings on theology, linguistics, liturgical rituals, and ecclesial history. Tonsured in 1874 by his uncle, Fr. Abdel Massih the Great, he gave himself over to intense studying, becoming fluent in Hebrew, Syriac, Greek, and Coptic. His most notable and significant work was the compiling of the Book of Holy Euchologion, *Kitāb Al-Khulājī Al-Muqaddas* (i.e., *Kitāb al-Thalāth Quddāsāt* [The Book of the Three Divine Liturgies]) in 1902.

in the Wilderness of the Jordan.

Hanna Henein, the youngest brother of Fr. Abdel Massih, describes:

He spent seven years in the Wilderness of John the Baptist and Mary of Egypt. [When he returned,] I asked him, "In those seven years in the Wilderness of John the Baptist, what were you eating?"

He told me, "Hanna, my brother, I only ate grass and weeds."

During his time in the region, he made a pilgrimage to the Holy Land four times.

By the end of his seventh year in the wilderness, the severity of his ascetic life had so weakened his body that ticks and other parasites fed upon his flesh. In this condition, he was no longer able to remain in the Wilderness of the Jordan. He therefore returned to Egypt and took up residence in the dependency[17] of the Monastery of St. Anthony the Great in the village of Boush, in Beni Suef.

Hanna continues:

When we heard that he had gone to the monastery at Boush, my uncle and I went to see him.

Fr. Hananiah, who was standing at the gate, asked me, "Who are you looking for?"

I said, "I want Fr. Abdel Massih. He is from the Monastery of St. Macarius."

---

17 A dependency refers to any building owned and maintained by a monastery that is located outside the monastery's main property. This can include churches, farmland, guesthouses for traveling monks, and other similar structures.

He took us to his room. When we opened the door, we found that he was sleeping in the storage shed! The room was filled with the monastery's supply of ghee and cheese, and it was also where they kept the broken furniture. Only a small corner remained empty, and that was where he slept.

Upon seeing him, Fr. Abdel Massih embraced his little brother and covered him with kisses; he had left him when he was only a newborn. He allowed him to spend the night there with him. Fr. Abdel Massih continued living in that room for nearly two years.

The monk, on one occasion, traveled to Abu Shehata and stayed in his family's home for three days. When the people of Manahra learned that the monk had returned from the desert, they came and took him with them to their village. There, he settled among them and began to minister to their spiritual needs.[18]

Though he felt a direct call from the Lord to serve the people, Fr. Abdel Massih desired nothing more than to conceal himself. The people sought him out, especially as his spiritual gifts began to manifest. He felt that his ministry in the world was not conducive to his desire to be hidden, for, as he would describe, people often ran after appearances and praised him.

He dreaded praise and actively fled from it, putting into deed the words of our Lord, "When you have done all those things which you are commanded, say, 'We are unprofitable servants.'"[19]

---

18   *A Talk of Memories: The Life and Miracles of Fr. Abdel Massih of Manahra* by Mr. Hanna, the Saint's Brother. Audio Recording

19   Lk 17:10.

One of the fathers at the monastery warned him, "At the moment virtue is revealed, it is stolen and robbed by vain glory."

When he began his ministry, he often ran to his spiritual fathers, burdened by the praise of men. They, in turn, instructed him, "If you cannot run away from men, make them run away from you."

*Fr. Yacoub al-Masudi ("the silent monk," left),
stands next to his brother, Fr. Abdel Massih Salib al-Masudi*

CHAPTER THREE

A Fool for Christ

How would he make men run away from him?

Under the guidance of the two brothers from the Monastery of Baramous, he decided to pursue a most difficult ascetic struggle, one which required a complete emptying of oneself: he would become a fool for Christ. His spiritual elders themselves often took this path, hiding their holiness behind the use of bizarre phrases and acts, feigning lapses in sanity.

In reading the account of his life and that of others like him, it would be easily and most simply believed that Fr. Abdel Massih was mentally unsound because of the way he interacted, spoke, and lived. However, it would later be well-established that he had always been in full and complete possession of his faculties, but cast them off publicly for Christ's sake.

Fr. Raphael, Fr. Pachom, and Fr. Salama, senior monks at the Monastery of St. Macarius, revealed the very first instance in which the monk needed to voluntarily pursue madness to escape vain glory, choosing to become a fool for Christ.

Pope Youannis XIX began to receive word about Fr. Abdel Massih, as his virtues began to be widely recognized. The Pope, at the time, was in search of a righteous father confessor, and so he summoned him. Upon further consideration, the patriarch decided within himself that it would be selfish to keep the monk to himself; he considered laying his hands on the monk's head, even if against his will, to ordain him a metropolitan.

Fr. Abdel Massih left the wilderness for Cairo, accepting the summons, though he was completely unaware of the Pope's plans. As he settled into a chair in the patriarch's reception hall, Fr. Abdel Massih found himself besieged with a barrage of compliments and praises coming from the Pope. The Pope was known for having a fondness for monasticism, and harbored a particular admiration for monks with noble reputations, but Fr. Abdel Massih truly struggled to endure the incessant stream of praises pouring from Pope

Pope Youannis XIX, the 113th Pope of Alexandria and Patriarch of the See of St. Mark, (1855–1942)

Youannis' lips. Though the patriarch's praises stemmed out of his love for the monks, Fr. Abdel Massih recoiled at hearing them. To make matters worse, the patriarch implied the subject of ordaining him.

Fearing lest vain glory begin to take root in him, he resolved to say something that would defy expectations, something unheard of for a man of his "reputation." In short, it was something quite daring to utter in the presence of anyone, let alone the patriarch himself.

"You're married to my mother," Fr. Abdel Massih interrupted, his voice cut through the air like a sharp blade.

Pope Youannis, stunned by such a claim, sat frozen. The words he just heard could not register. His features contorted with a combination of shock and disbelief. The patriarch's eyes widened in anger.

"I want to get married, too!" the monk added, adding fuel to an already kindled flame.

Pope Youannis gripped his staff tightly and yelled, standing from his seat, "Leave this place at once! I thought you were a saint, but now I see you are a madman!"

With a sense of relief flooding his heart, Fr. Abdel Massih instantly took leave of the papal residence. His spirit was immediately lifted by his escape from the burden of ordination; it surely would have jeopardized his salvation had he been ordained and failed in fulfilling the demands required of him.

The statement he blurted out, unbeknownst to the patriarch, actually held resonance: indeed, the pope was married to his mother—but not in the conventional sense. From the very instant of Pope Youannis' ascension to the throne, he had become spiritually betrothed to his mother, the Church; he was bound by a holy covenant that transcended all other unions.

From that moment onward, Fr. Abdel Massih continued feigning madness and folly, using this new demeanor to shield against people's praises.

Like many other fools for Christ, he would communicate in absurd riddles and shocking statements in order to instruct and portray truths that are much deeper than they appear. Fr. Abdel Massih frequently employed this enigmatic phrase in his charade of madness: "I want to get married." It was a stark contradiction to his solemn vow of celibacy, and naturally, it turned heads.

In reality, and as he told the patriarch, he truly did want to get married; with great longing did he await the day of his repose, in which he was to be wed to his Bridegroom, Christ.

This saying, being so misunderstood, among other sayings and riddles, served as a catalyst for widespread skepticism regarding his sanctity and, more significantly, his commitment to purity as a monk. As whispers of doubt murmured among those who surrounded him, the once-revered monastic found himself increasingly derided. Fr. Abdel Massih would bear this ill-treatment silently. His feigning of foolishness and his undeniably outlandish conduct would cause him to be ridiculed, abused, belittled, and scorned for the rest of his life.

Yet what he did was not strange; Christ Himself appeared as a fool to the world around Him—and does to this day. He lived as a poor carpenter, though He is God in the flesh. He willingly took upon Himself the most agonizing death sentence of Roman crucifixion, though He was without spot and blameless. In the eyes of the world, what could be more "foolish" than that? Even St. Paul speaks of this "irrationality:"

> For the message of the cross is foolishness to those who are perishing, but to us who are being saved it is the power of God. For it is written: "I will destroy the wisdom of the wise, And bring to nothing the understanding of the prudent." Where is the wise? Where is the scribe? Where is the disputer of this age? Has not God made foolish the wisdom of this world? For since, in the wisdom of God, the world through wisdom did not know God, it pleased God through the foolishness of the message preached to save those who believe. For Jews request a sign, and Greeks seek

after wisdom; but we preach Christ crucified, to the Jews a stumbling block and to the Greeks foolishness, but to those who are called, both Jews and Greeks, Christ the power of God and the wisdom of God. Because the foolishness of God is wiser than men, and the weakness of God is stronger than men.[20]

Christ our Lord accepted to Himself cruelty, mocking, and ultimately death, as He paved the way to the Father through Himself. Fr. Abdel Massih would also choose to bear ill-treatment and ridicule for Christ's sake. Of his own volition, he tarnished his reputation and brought upon himself the dark shadows of suspicion; and yet, he favored the disdain over the risk of sin. He desired to disappear. He desired to be last, to be forgotten.

I Want to Marry You!

Mother Kyria Wassef, the late abbess of the Convent of St. Philopater Mercurius in Old Cairo, explains a situation that occurred during the period in which Fr. Abdel Massih was assigned to hear the confessions of the nuns in the various convents of Old Cairo and Haret Zuweila.

Entering the Convent of St. Philopater Mercurius, he spotted a nun who pampered herself in all aspects of her life; she grew very particular in her food, favored only to wear cassocks[21] made with lavish fabrics, and often sought to

---

20   1 Cor 1:18–25.

21   A cassock is a long, robe-like garment traditionally worn by clergy, monastics, and seminarians in many Christian traditions. In the Coptic Orthodox Church, as well as other Eastern and Oriental Orthodox churches, the cassock, in the monastic context, is a visible sign of one's death to the world and consecration to Christ.

enhance her physical appearance. She forgot the asceticism and simplicity that accompany the monasticism she willingly chose for herself.

Fr. Abdel Massih, as her father confessor, wished to caution her. He spotted her from afar once and called her to himself.

"Mother," he smiled, "I want to marry you!"

As for the nun, she was taken aback and excused herself immediately, subsequently running away. His words disturbed her, and she began to fear him. She went to the abbess and related, in great embarrassment, what Fr. Abdel Massih told her: her father confessor had essentially proposed to her!

When she heard this, the abbess called three additional nuns. Together, they formulated a plan. In a room, a large, thick sheet would be hung up around a bed and draped in such a way as to reach the floor. This would allow the three nuns to hide behind it and eavesdrop while undetected. The nun accusing Fr. Abdel Massih was instructed to take him into the room under the guise of hearing her confession. There, his alleged indecency would be exposed.

With Fr. Abdel Massih visiting the convent once more, the plan was now in motion. He was led into the room and took a seat, not knowing that three other nuns hid in the very same room and listened on.

"Let's get married," the nun leaned in and whispered, according to the plan, "you and I."

"Leave this matter to tomorrow," he dismissed, hastily standing up, "we'll discuss then."

She began to insist, pulling his arm. "We're together now. Didn't you say you wanted to marry me?"

He responded, again, "Tomorrow."

The nun did not relent. She anticipated his immorality to be moments away from being publicized to the nuns overhearing the interaction. She wanted to expose him, and she would not take no for an answer. But her unremitting determination caused the monk to truly believe her advances were serious.

Fr. Abdel Massih's tone and manner of speech were completely altered. He was no longer the foolish, improper, failure of a monastic that many suspected him to be. He became the wise and holy elder he truly was.

He tightened his hold on the cross in his hand and rebuked her, "Shame on you! You're a nun! Preserve your body untainted, as well as your soul. The apostle says, 'Do you not know that you are the temple of God and that the Spirit of God dwells in you? If anyone defiles the temple of God, God will destroy him. For the temple of God is holy.'[22] And I am a monk, as well. The Lord would, without doubt, pour His wrath on us for breaking the vow of chastity we took on the day of our tonsure."

The nun's face became as pale as chalk. She sat stunned. He was the farthest thing from crazy.

He added, finally reproaching her, "And lest you be thrown in hell, dress yourself in humbler clothing. And cease from adorning yourself, for this is contrary to the life of monasticism."

He breathed deeply, concluding his admonition. He saw she was cut to the heart. Her tears of repentance began to join the conversation; she deeply lamented pampering herself and caring more for the beauty of her flesh than the beauty of her soul.

---

22   1 Cor 3:16–17.

It was here that he chose to return to his madness. But before he could utter another bizarre phrase to conceal himself, the nuns jumped out from behind the sheet and extolled, "We are witnesses [to your holiness], Fr. Abdel Massih!"

He stood his ground, wishing to confuse them, "I was going to marry her!"

But they could no longer be convinced. Each nun was ready to kiss his hands. Withdrawing in horror, he pledged, feigning anger, "I swear by my Lady the Virgin that I'll leave, and I won't sit with any of you ever again!"

He escaped the convent as fast as his feet could take him, fleeing their words of praise. He never entered the Convent of St. Philopater Mercurius again.

Metropolitan Mena commented, "Though he had the gift of clairvoyance, I believe the Lord hid the matter from him, not revealing the nuns' plan to him, in order to make his sanctity known to the entire convent."

Many may suppose that feigning madness to safeguard virtue is unbecoming, unacceptable, or even unholy. And yet the Church is rich with the examples of saints who took to acting the fool, and therefore accepted ridicule, in order to escape vain glory and pride. Their demeanor was favorably accepted by God as an act of self-denial, and their biographies testify to this.

St. Anna Simone was a queen who, taking off her crown and abdicating the throne after contemplating the vanity of the world, chose to act foolishly when she desired to dwell among nuns; she feigned mental illness, though she was in full command of her faculties. Consequently, the nuns dubbed her *Habila*—literally, dumb or stupid. She hid her sanctity until one night, at the time appointed by God, it was revealed that whenever she stood to pray, unearthly light emerged from her, and angels hovered around her. When the matter was revealed, she fled the convent and was never seen again.

Abba Fureij,[23] who reposed at the beginning of the fifteenth century, was a layman who voluntarily changed his name to "*Teji Eflīou*," translated from Coptic as Teji the liar or the madman. He often acted as such to avoid praise. As with many of these fools for Christ, he became a source of guidance and wonderworking, and was sought out for healing and prayers. And whenever a miracle was wrought by God at his hands, he often fled the village, going to another and changing his alias yet again.

These two examples, among many more, after choosing this ascetic path, were later revealed to have reached unbelievable levels of holiness, all veiled under this fabricated madness.

Nevertheless, Fr. Abdel Massih's biographer emphasizes an incredibly crucial point:

> While this approach may be suitable to some, it is not universally applicable, nor is it conducive to the edification of the Church. We do not advocate following this path. Otherwise, the Church in its entirety would be full of fools and madmen.[24]

Marry Me Off

In one instance, Fr. Abdel Massih visited Manahra in early 1957, and upon entering the church, he noticed a certain elderly woman named Mustafiya sitting in one of the pews.

---

23   Or it may be spelled as Furaij.

24   The Arabic Life of Fr. Abdel Massih, 24.

"Her," he turned to Fr. Luka of St. Macarius,[25] nodding in her direction, "marry me off to that woman."

He was insistent. Fr. Abdel Massih went as far as urging Fr. Luka to schedule a visit to her house so the three can decide on a wedding date. Even worse, he pressed Fr. Youhanna Suleiman al-Abawani, the village priest, to draft an official marriage certificate for him and Mustafiya.

As for the apparent bride, who would die of old age within a few years after this incident, she was familiar with the monk's ways and sat unbothered.

Fr. Youhanna found himself in a nervous sweat. He relayed the distressing turn of events to Fr. Luka. Little did he know the latter was, unfortunately, already involved.

"If the metropolitan gets news of this," Fr. Youhanna stammered, "we'll all get defrocked! I don't know whether to believe him or not!"

Fr. Luka tried to offer a way out. "Do you have an old, expired marriage certificate?" he asked. "Bring it. Let's see where this charade leads."

Fr. Youhanna remembered a book of outdated certificates he had once entrusted to the church steward. He and a deacon named Saleeb Wahba went to retrieve the book. The intention was to fill out a marriage license on one of the expired forms, just convincing enough to satisfy him.

With the certificates in hand, they approached Fr. Abdel Massih's room and were about to knock. The door was cracked open; what they saw from within the cell would completely immobilize them.

---

25   Later to become Metropolitan Mena of Girga, the biographer of Fr. Abdel Massih.

The monk they believed to be senseless and immoral was seen standing in prayer with his hands extended upward. Each of his dark, slender fingers was casting a luminous beam of light with a radiant glow and intensity likened to that of an electric lamp.

It was 9:00 a.m. And yet the miraculous light emanating from his fingers overpowered the sunshine coming through the window. The room was completely engulfed. The miraculous spectacle rendered them speechless with awe. Saleeb and Fr. Youhanna took turns peering through the door in order to confirm that their eyes were not deceiving them.

Fr. Abdel Massih's fingers were, in fact, emanating light.

Fr. Youhanna, previously apprehensive, was now unequivocally terrified.

He went to Fr. Luka, shaking and frightened, explaining to him what he and Saleeb had just witnessed. Still, Fr. Abdel Massih insisted on continuing with his "performance," and they all began to believe he was serious, in spite of what occurred in his cell.

Fr. Abdel Massih's spiritual son, Makram, was brought as a last resort.

"Makram, please," Fr. Luka pleaded, tugging at his arm, "you know the man better than any of us. Get us out of this mess!"

Fr. Luka's relationship with Fr. Abdel Massih was only in its beginning stages at this point, so Makram intervened. He fabricated an excuse.

"*Father*" he began calmly, taking a seat and putting his arm around him, "the government just passed a new regulation. Anyone issuing a marriage certificate now has to be officially registered with the authorities. Neither Fr. Luka nor Fr. Youhanna is on the registry yet. So unfortunately, they're not allowed to officiate."

He glared at all of them, pretending to be furious. Standing up and swiftly clutching his walking stick, he yelled, "You're all here to tease me! You want to ruin my wedding! Give me the money I paid. I'm not getting married anymore!"

And so, he ended his performance.

The Liturgy Stopped

The same Makram, narrating the following incident, explains that he once stood at the altar during the Liturgy, serving as a deacon alongside Fr. Abdel Massih, and they reached the moment of the Epiclesis.[26]

In the middle of his sentence, Fr. Abdel Massih fell silent. The prayers were abruptly halted. Kneeling beside the altar, Makram glanced upward from the ground to find Fr. Abdel Massih in a state of complete dissociation, his gaze fixed heavenward. He had entered into a trance-like state, lost in a vision he was witnessing.

The Liturgy stopped for a full five minutes. Everyone remained in total silence. Growing restless, Makram and *Moallem*[27] Girgis attempted to redirect Fr. Abdel Massih's

---

26   This Greek word, which means to summon or invoke, is a liturgical invocation where the priest requests that the Holy Spirit descend upon the bread and wine that they mysteriously become the Lord's Body and Blood.

27   The title *Moallem* typically refers to a respected or knowledgeable person who serves as a teacher, mentor, or leader within the Egyptian community. In Coptic ecclesial contexts, the *Moallem* is entrusted with teaching the coming generations the hymns and rites of the Church, along with the liturgical cues and rudimentary Coptic language.

focus back to the prayers. Despite their efforts—gesturing to the book to indicate the place he stopped at, whispering the litanies he was to chant next—he remained unresponsive. He paid them no attention.

Then, in a sudden and startling turn of events, they witnessed a brilliant and overpowering light erupt just above the Sacrifice. It then intensified, expanding and completely submerging the entire sanctuary in light.

Overwhelmed with fear, Makram cried out, "Look, Moallem!"

But Moallem Girgis, in great distress, struggled to articulate a single word. After a few moments of stammering and stuttering, his tongue was finally loosened, and he exclaimed in awe, "I see, Makram! I see!"

Through the intense brightness of the heavenly light, they were able to discern Fr. Abdel Massih beginning to weep. He started to beat his chest and silently shake his head.

At the conclusion of the service, he sought to divert attention away from the extraordinary scene witnessed by everyone. He loudly declared in the presence of the congregation, in a bid to scandalize and shock them, "I'm angry with you, O Virgin! Why would you reveal my secret before the people?"

The people swarmed him. He, however, forcefully pushed his way through the crowd, making his way to the door. He shouted, looking to the assembly of the faithful behind him, "Go find another priest for yourselves! I'm angry with the Virgin!"

From that day forward, he refrained from praying in that parish.

Fr. Abdel Massih, of course, could not put himself at odds with the Blessed Theotokos,[28] for he would rejoice at the mere mentioning of her name. Nor could he put himself at odds with the altar itself. Rather, he said such things because he harbored a deep concern: the possibility of the recurrence of such a situation in the future. He feared lest those in the surrounding area might know the truth about him, and hence divert his focus from deepening his relationship with the Lord.

Compelled to Reveal the Truth

Metropolitan Mena writes that in 1977, shortly after his arrival in Manahra for seclusion, he paid a visit to a woman named Roum Tawfiq of Manahra upon learning of her illness. Apart from inquiring about her well-being, he seized the opportunity to gather further insight as he began preparing to write Fr. Abdel Massih's biography. Roum lived in a house directly opposite the chicken coop, which served as the makeshift cell of the monk. He was convinced that she was a witness to the most remarkable things.

She recounted that, one day, she passed by Fr. Abdel Massih's room, which had a small window about a meter and a half from the ground. Curiosity compelled her to peek inside. She saw him sleeping on the floor.

Suddenly, and to her astonishment, a radiant light burst forth from his face, resembling that of a light bulb. Then, his ten fingers emitted rays of fiery light like ten candles. Overwhelmed by fear, she hastily walked away.

---

28   The Greek Θεοτόκος, meaning "one who gives birth to God," commonly translated as "Mother of God," is used universally in the Orthodox Church to refer to the Holy Virgin Mary, affirming that she is the Mother of God the Son, the Lord Jesus, who is both fully God and fully human.

Approximately thirty minutes later, she revisited the spot only to find Fr. Abdel Massih had emerged from the cell. He quickly sealed off the window with bricks so no one would see him, whether he prayed or slept.

Initially, she says that she vowed to keep silent about what she saw. However, when she heard the explanation he began to spread as to why he decided to seal the window—that snakes and frogs found their way into his room through it—she felt compelled to reveal the truth to others.

The Window was Open

Mariam, the wife of Hanna Youaqim of Manahra, adds to the above testaments by relating how, on one night, she descended from the upper floor of their house to attend to some chores. As she crossed the hallway, she found herself passing by the guest room, where Fr. Abdel Massih was spending the night.

The window of the room was open halfway, and her curiosity beckoned her to steal a glance inside. She saw Fr. Abdel Massih standing in prayer, his arms stretched toward heaven. He was surrounded by a halo of strong heavenly light. The entire room was bathed in an unearthly glow.

Overcome by a sudden impulse, she called out, "Remember me in your prayers, Fr. Abdel Massih!"

In response, he turned to her and pretended, as usual, to be crazy and insane.

His Almsgiving

All of Manahra's inhabitants are witnesses to Fr. Abdel Massih's extraordinary generosity to the poor, despite what little he himself owned. He had a "unique" approach to almsgiving.

To illustrate, he would gather the local children and orphans from the streets, "Come, come work with me! I want to hire you!"

Familiar with his unconventional methods, three or four boys would eagerly follow him to his cell, thrilled to be "employed" by the monk.

Once the children assembled outside the cell, he assigned them a task: "I want you to look for the tempters," he instructed, "let us see if they are lurking around."

The children, accompanied by their peculiar employer, scoured the surrounding area for demons for five minutes. Obviously, none were found; it was all an excuse to give them money.

He then took them back to his cell, "Say, 'the black beggar of a monk!'"

They repeated after him, as ordered, but in hushed tones; they were reluctant to speak such insulting words about Fr. Abdel Massih. He then handed each of the poor boys a coin, "Take your wages and go home, since [the tempters] are not around."

Moallem Girgis, the head deacon of the church of St. Mary in Manahra, recalls that whenever Fr. Abdel Massih, by the Spirit, would sense that he was in want, he would call him to himself and say, "Come, Girgis. Pass through this small canal and look for the tempters."

The canal the monk directed him to was roughly a meter deep and two meters wide. Taking off his tunic, Girgis would descend into the water, pass to the other side, and then return to him.

"So? Have you found them?"

"I can't find them," Girgis shrugged, looking up to him

from the canal.

He would extend his hand and hand him the sum he needed at the time. "Take your wages and go home," he smiled, "since the tempters are not around."

Girgis instantly recognized Fr. Abdel Massih's intent behind ordering him to do what he did; the two had a friendship that spanned twenty years, so he understood him well. He sought to offer Girgis aid while concealing his charity beneath the guise of foolishness. Those around him had misconceptions regarding why he did such things, believing he foolishly scattered whatever money he received without appreciation. And yet, Fr. Abdel Massih did this deliberately to hide his virtues. People never understood him.

An Attempt to Seduce Him

He employed his guise of insanity not only to avoid praise but to evade temptation, sometimes to life-threatening degrees.

A priest, contemporary of Fr. Abdel Massih, narrates a most perilous episode in the life of the monk. A young woman invited Fr. Abdel Massih to her apartment for a home blessing prayer. She led the way to a three-story building, where she inhabited a small room on the top floor. The moment the two of them walked through the door, the woman brazenly solicited the monk to sin with her. He vehemently rejected each of her advances and sought to leave the apartment immediately.

She seized him forcefully from the collar of his worn-out tunic, and being physically stronger than he was, she attempted to force him onto her bed.

Fr. Abdel Massih, discerning the gravity of the situation, cried out, "Get away from me!"

He managed to break free of her grip, considering the window by the mattress his only refuge. The monk lunged forward and hurled himself out of the window, falling into the street three stories below.

The woman looked on in terror. She screamed as she saw the monk plummet to his death, and yet Fr. Abdel Massih arose from the ground completely unscathed. He dusted off his tunic, hastily ran back to his cell, and slammed the door behind him.

The priest who conveyed this story added that this woman, seeing how the Lord rescued Fr. Abdel Massih from what was certainly a fatal fall, grew extremely remorseful and repented of her attempt to seduce him. Following a sincere confession, she became renewed and lived the rest of her days in purity.

Metropolitan Mena further attests, "I became aware of several situations similar to this story repeating with the saint with more than one woman, and in more than one place. Each time, he would escape using his acts of madness, thus saving himself from spiritual ruin."[29]

His Living Conditions

He did not possess more than one tunic at a time. His disciples confirm that, during their frequent visits to his cell, they did not see a single article of clothing lying around, besides the one he used to cover himself.

Also, in speaking of the condition of his tunic, it was collectively agreed upon that, if he had thrown it into the street, no one would choose to take it, even if they had need of it. The only reason one would desire to take it would be for

---

29   The Arabic Life of Fr. Abdel Massih, 41–42.

a blessing. Metropolitan Mena was able to acquire for himself such a tunic, which he later placed in the shrine by Fr. Abdel Massih's body.

He would break off a branch from a tree, or pull a frond from a palm, and fashion it into a simple walking stick. He did this often, and many of these sticks he later left with his spiritual children, who in turn passed them down. To this day, many families in Manahra cherish owning one of his humble canes, preserving them as relics in their homes.

He rarely bathed, being more focused on his prayers than on the needs of his flesh. In spite of this, he constantly exuded a sweet-smelling fragrance, both from his clothing and his body.

His cell in Manahra was a dilapidated chicken coop, serving as a hermitage, built from adobe bricks of the poorest condition. It was not painted. In truth, it was the most run-down place, a place only the poorest and most impoverished would force themselves to inhabit—no, even lowlier than them.

The cell, which at a point in time partially collapsed because of humidity and excessive groundwater, was restored by the metropolitan to preserve the memory of the holy monk who once occupied it.

The tunic, turban, and walking sticks of Fr. Abdel Massih

CHAPTER FOUR

The Anchoritic Life

Before delving into the many documented accounts proving his inclusion among the Spirit-borne anchorites, the Arabic biography of Fr. Abdel Massih incorporates a detailed preface about the often-misunderstood anchorites themselves. This preface, penned by his biographer, Metropolitan Mena, explores the unique characteristics of these desert fathers. Metropolitan Mena "sheds light" on the mysteries surrounding them, outlining their ascetic practices, their relationship with God, and their blessed interactions with one another.[30]

Through this comprehensive depiction, a deeper understanding is gained about not only Fr. Abdel Massih's life, but also, in a broader context, about that of the anchorites.

Who are the Anchorites?

Before I begin sharing the testimonies of those who have seen [Fr. Abdel Massih] as an anchorite, or [his] praying with the anchorites, I find it necessary to shed light on the truth behind the anchorite fathers themselves, as explained by those who verified [this truth]. And so, we say:

---

30   This chapter is taken from The Arabic Life of Fr. Abdel Massih, 32–36, translated by the author.

The anchorites are an undeniable fact. They are humans like us, and through their spiritual struggle, they have reached lofty levels of sanctity, so the Lord has graciously granted them the gifts of anchoritic abilities; their own guardian angels carrying them to wheresoever they desire, or if they wish to gather together.

They commonly dwell in caves [in the desert]. They feed on the herbs, which sprout from the rain, or grass, or plants near the mountains. They travel individually or in groups.

There are at least three participants who assemble to celebrate the Divine Liturgy: one prays as the priest, the second is a deacon, and the third is a cantor.

They dress in pieces of coarse fabric or sheep's wool sewn together, merely [for the purpose of] covering their nakedness. To some, God grants that their hair may grow to the extent of covering their entire bodies. They do not feel the cold of winter, nor the heat of summer, if the Lord so provides this for them.

They must gather [for prayer] on the eve of Sunday, around midnight, and they conclude near sunrise. Some of them gird themselves with a girdle of iron. Some of them dwell close to people, yet, in their souls, they are far from them all.

Biblical Proof

In the fourteenth chapter of the Book of Daniel (verses 29–42 LXX), from the Deuterocanonical books:

> So they came to the king and said, "Deliver us Daniel, or else we will destroy you and your house." Now when the king saw that they pressed him sore, being constrained, he delivered Daniel to them, who cast him into the lions' den, where he was six days. And in the den there were seven lions, and they had

given them every day two carcasses and two sheep, which then were not given to them, to the intent they might devour Daniel. Now there was a prophet called Habakkuk, who had made pottage and had broken bread in a bowl, and was going into the field to bring it to the reapers. But the angel of the Lord said to Habakkuk, "Go, carry the dinner that you have into Babylon to Daniel, who is in the lions' den." And Habakkuk said, "Lord, I never saw Babylon; neither do I know where the den is." Then the angel of the Lord took him by the crown, and carried him by the hair of his head, and through the vehemency of his spirit set him in Babylon over the den. And Habakkuk cried, saying, "O Daniel, Daniel, take the dinner which God has sent you." And Daniel said, "You have remembered me, O God: neither have You forsaken them that seek You and love You." So Daniel arose and did eat, and the angel of the Lord set Habakkuk in his own place again immediately. Upon the seventh day the king went to bewail Daniel, and when he came to the den, he looked in, and behold, Daniel was sitting. Then cried the king with a loud voice, saying, "Great is the Lord God of Daniel, and there is none other beside You." And he drew him out, and cast those that were the cause of his destruction into the den, and they were devoured in a moment before his face.

And in the book of 1 Kings 18:7–12:

Now as Obadiah was on his way, suddenly Elijah met him; and he recognized him, and fell on his face, and said, "Is that you, my lord Elijah?" And he answered him, "It is I. Go, tell your master, 'Elijah is here.'" So he said, "How have I sinned, that you are delivering your servant into the hand of Ahab, to kill me? As the

Lord your God lives, there is no nation or kingdom where my master has not sent someone to hunt for you; and when they said, 'He is not here,' he took an oath from the kingdom or nation that they could not find you. And now you say, 'Go, tell your master, "Elijah is here"'! And it shall come to pass, as soon as I am gone from you, that the Spirit of the Lord will carry you to a place I do not know.

In Acts 8:39:

Now when they came up out of the water, the Spirit of the Lord caught Philip away, so that the eunuch saw him no more; and he went on his way rejoicing.

Historical Proof

It was written of St. Anthony that a cloud would carry him to cities and great distances away. St. Macarius, when traveling and growing tired, would be transported by God miraculously.

Also, the Church remembers many of these anchorite fathers. For example, to name a few: Abba Paul [the First Hermit], commemorated by the Church on the second of Meshir; Abba Timothy the Anchorite, commemorated by the Church on the 23rd of Koiahk, as well as Abba Misael, commemorated on the 13th of Koiahk; St. Mary of Egypt, commemorated by the Church on the 6th of Paremhotep, along with St. Zosima the Anchorite; St. Onuphrius the Anchorite, commemorated by the Church on the 16th of Paone, among others like Abba Pigimi, Abba Paphnutius, Abba Karas, and Abba Moses the Anchorite.[31]

---

31   For further reading on the lives of the anchorites of early Christian monasticism, see *The Hermit Fathers* by Fr. Samaan of the Monastery of the Syrians.

The Writings of Others

When Mr. Hassan al-Ashmawy, the attorney and member of the Muslim Brotherhood, was sought for arrest, he fled into the desert in 1954, walking a journey that spanned three and a half hours. In his memoir, which was published in the book *al-ʾIkhwan wa-l-Thawra* [The Brotherhood and the Revolution], printed in 1977, he writes verbatim:

Life in the desert did not solely consist of being surrounded by death, or hardship that suffocates the soul, or the experience of being deprived of everything. I found in it a great deal of profound pleasure and deep comfort. In it were long moments of contemplation and clarity of soul.

In it also was the friendliness of the spirits and ghosts; they called out, sang, materialized, and vanished. [With them,] I felt a sense of acceptance for my setting; it was this that gave me the contemplation I needed to sit down and write. O how much was written while in that place in the desert! Most of my writings, though, I have burned. As for what remains, I hid there. However, I believe the time has approached for me to unearth what I have concealed from its hiding place.

The subject of spirits and ghosts is something I have attempted to keep to myself, fearing that people would put my sanity into serious question. Personally, I do not consider myself to have the clairvoyance that mystics speak of. I still sincerely find difficulty in believing what I have heard and seen. But it did happen.

So, as I mention it today, I simply recount what occurred without explanation, for I lack a clear interpretation of the things I have witnessed.

The role of spirits and ghosts in my life began a few days following my arrival in the desert. The nights in December were long, bitterly cold, and lonely. Whatever sleep I had was little because I could not grow accustomed to the place, nor did I find any comfort where I was. My mind was preoccupied with my current situation, [as well as] the fate of my family, and that of my colleagues.

It was an extremely cold night. A fierce wind blew from the valley into the desert, and the darkness seemed infinite. The sky was covered with clouds, and yet they offered me absolutely no hope of rain. The darkness was so overwhelming that I could barely have seen my hand had I withdrawn it from under the covers.

Suddenly, a sound arose; it gave me the impression that a group of people had gathered together.

What followed was a beautiful voice singing a hymn. The singing continued for a full hour. A chorus of voices occasionally joined in, singing in response. The voices then quieted down, and then the chanting ceased completely. I heard all of this.

It seemed like something that could be explained logically—the wind must have carried the sounds of a celebration from the villages nearby, allowing them to reach me. That rationalization instantly failed when I remembered that the desert was a three and a half hour's walk from civilization.

In the quiet of the night, with the wind blowing, a whistling could be heard through the desert valleys. It was then that the sounds would return—the calls, the gathering, and the chanting, with the chorus answering. Eventually, the sounds would quiet down, and the chanting would stop.

In the beginning, I was perplexed, but then I supposed that the wind, along with the silence and isolation, must have created for me an illusion of calling, singing, and chanting. It was just the wind, [I thought,] whistling through the valleys and between the hills. This deceived my isolated mind into interpreting it in a way that brought me solace and tranquility.

And so, nights went by. There were no winds. A breeze neither blew from the east nor from the west. Yet the sound came back for a third time—the calling, the gathering, the chanting, and the chorus's responses. Again, little by little, the sounds grew quiet and faded away.

This time, I now had no explanation other than that these were hallucinations caused by my loneliness, isolation, and anxiety.

And yet, did my mind really falter?

The sounds kept visiting the place at least once a week, lasting until just before dawn, never leaving me for a single day. I found companionship in [the sounds]… I memorized words [from the chanting], that I never heard or read in my life. What I heard was reality, though I know nothing of its source.

I divulged to Sheikh Ahmed about what I had heard before he passed away. He explained to me that these were spirits wandering in the place. If I stayed long enough and got used to them, he continued, I might have seen them physically appear before me.

I did not argue with him. Nor did I believe, or deny, his words. After hearing his opinion, I kept what I experienced in the desert hidden from others.

My stay in the wilderness grew longer, and I became accustomed to the sounds of the spirits. Eventually, as my time in the wilderness was reaching its end, I began to see these ghosts wandering about when the singing [began], and yet their features still remained indistinct to me.[32]

There is no doubt that Hassan al-Ashmawi is truthful in what he wrote. He describes having heard voices, chanting, singing, and the response of the chorus, a line of chanters. He understood some things, remembered certain words, but had no explanation for the source of it all.

It is obvious that one cannot discern clear chanting and hymns, as well as a chorus's responses to one another, because of the wind whistling through the desert. The sure reality of what Hassan al-Ashmawi attempted to explain, as much as he could, is this: the "spirits" and "ghosts" he encountered are surely the Spirit-borne anchorites, whom God has given these gifts to.

I know someone honest, truthful, who prefers that his name not be mentioned, who admits to having prayed the Divine Liturgy with the saintly anchorites. He himself was the leading presbyter, and he communed them of the Holy Mysteries, for an ordained priest was not numbered among them; the anchorite priest who was with them had recently departed to Paradise. For this reason, they took this person

---

32   Hassan al-Ashmawi, *Al-ʾIkhwan wa-l-Thawra* [The Brotherhood and the Revolution], 1977, 139–141.

with them so that he might raise the Sacrifice for them and give them Communion.

He relayed that he did not know how he was taken with them to the heart of the desert. He also told me that after the distribution [of the Holy Eucharist], he was transported back to his village the same way he left it. They left him with promises and commands which he refuses to reveal.

The Testimony of Pope Kyrillos VI

The year was 1957. Fr. Luka of the Monastery of St. Macarius travelled to Manahra to visit his spiritual father, Fr. Abdel Massih. The two sat on the ground in the cell and conversed for a while, and then Fr. Luka stood up, excusing himself to catch his train to Cairo.

"You're going to Cairo?" Fr. Abdel Massih asked, "Take this with you."

He dug into the pocket of his tunic and pulled out a sealed envelope, extending it to Fr. Luka.

"Tell them it is from Fr. Abdel Massih of St. Macarius, the fool."

The envelope, he explained, contained a written message for Fr. Mansour of Baramous,[33] who, at the time, resided in Old Cairo with Fr. Mena the Recluse. On his arrival in Cairo, Fr. Luka found the renowned Fr. Mena sitting in the simple reception hall, with him Fr. Makary of the Monastery of the Syrians.[34]

---

33   Fr. Mansour would be ordained Metropolitan of the Diocese of Gharbiya, Beheira, and Qafr al-Sheikh on December 13, 1959, taking the name Metropolitan Isaac.

34   Hegumen Fr. Makary would be ordained General Bishop of Ecumenical Services on September 30, 1962, taking the name Bishop Samuel.

Fr. Luka's knowledge of Fr. Mena the Recluse, at the time, was limited; they had only heard of one another in passing. He sat in the reception hall and asked him about the whereabouts of Fr. Mansour.

"I have a message for him from Fr. Abdel Massih of St. Macarius, the fool," Fr. Luka said, showing him the envelope.

At the mere mention of his name, Fr. Mena grew remarkably excited, "Where is he? Is Fr. Abdel Massih still alive until now?"

"Yes, my father, he is alive and in good health."

He asked, more eager than before, leaning in, "And where is he now?"

"In Manahra, district of Matai."

Fr. Mena sat back in his seat and smiled. "May his blessings be with us."

Here, Fr. Luka questioned, "Do you know him, my father?"

He answered, "I know him well, and I know many things about him. I was discipled unto him when he lived at the Monastery of Baramous."

Fr. Luka entreated Fr. Mena to share one of the things he came to know about Fr. Abdel Massih, admitting that he was often puzzled by that man; at times he thought Fr. Abdel Massih was the most rational human he had ever encountered, and sometimes he thought he really was crazy, and was not pretending to be so.

"Fr. Luka," Fr. Mena replied in a serious tone, "Fr. Abdel Massih is a great saint, but he disguises himself as a fool. He is one of the anchorites and constantly prays with them.

"I will tell you something I, myself, witnessed: One night,

I was baking the *Qorban*.[35] Fr. Abdel Massih lived with us [at the time] in the Monastery of Baramous. I got up to see if the bread had risen already, and it was around midnight. And I needed to walk past his cell.

"Passing by, I heard many voices inside his cell chanting the hymns of the Midnight Praises in a melodious and comforting tone. My curiosity led me to approach the door of his cell; I attempted to look between the wooden planks of the door to see which of the monks was praying with him.

"A brilliant, consuming, radiant light completely filled the cell; the light was not comparable to anything else in the monastery. The matter confused me. I wondered, 'Did the monks leave their cells and come to pray the Midnight Praises with Fr. Abdel Massih?'

"At long last, curiosity got the better of me, and I could resist no longer. I knocked on the door. The lights immediately went out. The voices vanished. Darkness overtook the cell. Fr. Abdel Massih emerged. Pretending to have been woken up, he rubbed his eyes vigorously as if to clear the sleep from them.

"'I'm asleep,' he yawned, pretending to be annoyed. 'Is it proper to disturb me while I'm resting? Is this monastic etiquette?'

"'I have sinned, my father,' I responded, thoroughly unconvinced. 'Absolve me.'

"'God absolve you. Don't do it again.' I walked away from him. Yet my curiosity struck me again with great intensity.

"I distanced myself from his cell, and finding a palm tree

---

35   The common practice in monasteries, to this day, is that the loaves of bread from which one is chosen for use in the Mystery of Eucharist, called Qorban, are baked by the monks themselves during the night, shortly before the beginning of the Divine Liturgy.

before me, I hid behind it, hoping to see which monks would emerge from his cell after chanting with him. I carefully observed till the monastery bell rang at 2:00 a.m., summoning the monks to gather for Midnight Praises.

"He came out alone and walked to the church. No one else followed him out. Ensuring he was gone, I instantly entered his cell, which he always left unlocked. I found nothing inside except the mat he slept on.

"For several nights, I observed his cell to confirm my suspicions. I heard the same voices on most nights, and saw the same radiant light through the wooden planks of the cell door, as I had before. Nevertheless, in obedience to his command, I did not dare to knock again. The scene recurred numerous times. I concluded, with all confidence, that Fr. Abdel Massih was praying with the Spirit-borne anchorites."[36]

Fr. Mena the Recluse (later Pope Kyrillos VI) (left)
Fr. Luka of the Monastery of St. Macarius (later Metropolitan Mena) (right)

---

36   The Arabic Life of Fr. Abdel Massih, 37–39.

The Testimony of a Monk Who Saw Him Flying

In 1960, Fr. Mikhail, an Ethiopian elder who took residence in the Monastery of the Syrians,[37] vividly remembers how Fr. Abdel Massih was also residing in the same monastery at the time. On one occasion, they both went on a short leave.[38]

At the end of their leave, each of the monks decided to take a different route back to Scetis; Fr. Mikhail traveled back to the monastery by a route from the city of Khatatba. He was accompanied by a caravan that was delivering provisions of food and supplies to the monastery.

For five hours, the caravan trekked through the desert on camels. Growing fatigued, Fr. Mikhail and the men in the caravan decided to rest; they dismounted from the camels and pack animals and sat on the sand to have lunch.

As Fr. Mikhail ate his food, his eyes caught a bird flying in their direction. The bird, which looked like a black crow, soared at a height of about a hundred meters above the ground, approximately a kilometer away from the caravan. The bird began to slowly descend till it landed on the sand and began to walk.

The distance, though it kept him from fully making out what he was observing, did not prevent him from fixing his gaze on the scene. He could not take his eyes off the sight before him.

---

37 Located in the Wilderness of Scetis, the Monastery of the Syrians (Arabic: *Dayr al-Suryan*) has roots dating back to the sixth century. The monastery is dedicated to, and named after, the Holy Theotokos, and yet is widely known by the name "of the Syrians" due to it being predominantly inhabited by Syriac Orthodox monks from the eighth to the fourteenth century.

38 Monks often had the option to make a pilgrimage or spend a brief period of retreat at another monastery or church.

The closer this mysterious object approached, the clearer it became, and the greater Fr. Mikhail's anticipation grew. The distance between them was now only a matter of meters.

The view finally cleared. It was Fr. Abdel Massih.

"Fr. Abdel Massih," he called out, shocked more than he could possibly imagine, "where did you come from?"

Feigning extreme exhaustion and pretending to have walked the entire distance, he groaned, "I came all the way from Khatatba."

Impulsively, Fr. Mikhail replied, "Fr. Abdel Massih, I saw you flying in the air and coming towards us! Remember me in your prayers!"

"You black Ethiopian!" He screamed, pretending to be furious, "You saw me flying?! Well, I'm not sitting with you all!"

Turning around, he stormed off into the desert, walking back in the direction of Khatatba until Fr. Mikhail and the men with him could no longer see him. Fr. Mikhail and the caravan mounted their animals and headed east, another five hours to the Monastery of the Syrians, while Fr. Abdel Massih walked westward until he disappeared into the horizon.

Walking through the gates of the Monastery of the Syrians, they all found Fr. Abdel Massih already there. Fr. Mikhail was shocked, and so he asked the monks about the timing of his arrival.

"About five hours ago," they told him. That is, moments after Fr. Abdel Massih disappeared from their sight, he was instantly caught away to the monastery. Fr. Mikhail came to know he was one of the Spirit-borne anchorites.

When asked whether he was upset with Fr. Abdel Massih after he called him a "black Ethiopian," Fr. Mikhail responded,

"Fr. Abdel Massih is no stranger to me. I understand him well. He did not insult me. He just used this method, which outwardly seemed offensive, to evade us and escape our questions."[39]

I'm Not Going

Moussa Abdel Malak worked for a wealthy cotton merchant from Samalut named Yacoub Bibawy. One evening, Yacoub called Moussa and told him to go at once to Manahra with his personal driver. He instructed Moussa to tell Fr. Abdel Massih that he was urgently needed in Samalut.

That same day, Moussa and the driver set out and traveled the fifteen and a half miles to Manahra, intending to bring Fr. Abdel Massih back to meet Yacoub.

Moussa and the driver parked by the Ibrahimiya Canal, and exiting the car, they found Fr. Abdel Massih sitting by the canal with his spiritual son, Makram, and a few other villagers.

Before they approached him, Fr. Abdel Massih turned around and yelled at Moussa, "What do you want? I'm not coming with you!"

Those with the monk, upon knowing they drove specifically to take him, implored Fr. Abdel Massih to go with them. He, however, completely refused. No reason was given whatsoever.

They left him sitting with them, returned to the car, and travelled all the way back to Samalut, directly to Yacoub's office, to inform him that Fr. Abdel Massih declined to go with them.

---

39   The Arabic Life of Fr. Abdel Massih, 39–40.

When they arrived at the office in Samalut, and passed through the entrance, they found Fr. Abdel Massih already in the doorway, walking ahead of them and taking a seat in front of Yacoub's desk!

Moussa attempted to relay everything to Yacoub: how Fr. Abdel Massih completely refused to ride with them in the car, how they pleaded with him—to no avail—and how he made it to the office before them!

"Stay quiet," Mr. Yacoub said, understanding the situation, "don't concern yourself with all of this."

The Wonderworking Monk

The Lord's gifts, including those of wonderworking, clairvoyance, and prophecy, become just one of many means by which His servants minister to the world. The apostles of Christ, being equipped with all manner of gifts, have not only cast out demons, but have cast out wickedness from the hearts of the people. The sicknesses of the flesh were indeed wondrously remedied, but more so the sicknesses of souls. They have not only done away with bodily blindness, but have also cured the blindness in innumerable souls.

Even presently, the Lord continues to freely grant His gifts to those who have chosen to ascend to Him, choosing to trample on the world. The wonders accomplished by God at the hands of Fr. Abdel Massih are in truth comparable to those accomplished at the hands of the apostles and the saints in the early centuries of the Church.

Metropolitan Mena writes:

It is without doubt that our father St. Abdel Massih was granted the gift of prophecy, knowledge of the hidden matters, and the working of wonders and miracles, as you will see. It can be said with all certainty that the description used by the Spiritual

Elder[40] applies to him: that the Lord reveals to them the deep past and what will [come to pass] in the distant future. In truth, this description applies fully to our holy father, for when you examine his miracles, you will find that most of them are connected to prophecies and the knowledge of hidden things, foretelling events long before they occurred.

Here we will present the prophecies in order, followed by the miracles. Not a single prophecy or miracle was written here except after it was heard directly from those who received the blessing of the saint themselves, or from those who personally witnessed the miracle. This was done so as to avoid any error in recounting what happened. [The miracles] have been recorded with complete honesty and accuracy.[41]

---

40   John of Dalyatha, also known as John Saba (c. 690–780), was a Syriac monk near the Turkey–Iraq border. After spending seven years in the monastery of Mar Yozadaq in the Qardu mountains, he withdrew to the 9,000-foot peaks of Beth Dalyatha, living most of his life in solitude. In old age he formed a community around himself and composed ascetic writings, which circulated anonymously and were translated into Arabic and Ethiopic, and later Latin.

41   The Arabic Life of Fr. Abdel Massih, 44.

A historical view of the church of St. Mary in Manahra,
as it stood during the lifetime of Fr. Abdel Massih

The Tall Recluse Becomes Pope

Metropolitan Mena remembers:

I was on a visit to the saint in the village of Manahra—and this was after the departure of Pope Yusab II—with the intention to confess, and to inform him of a voice I heard while I was in a state between wakefulness and sleep. It came to me three times, and it concerned the pope who was to come.

The voice told me, "Dwell not concerning the patriarch who is to come, for it is Mena the Recluse."

This came to pass only after I had raised long prayers, so that the Lord would select the pope from among the monks, per the canons of the Church.

When I arrived at [the cell of] our saintly father, I told him, "Fr. Abdel Massih, I heard a voice concerning the next pope."

Before I mentioned to him anything about what I heard, he interrupted me and said, "He is the patriarch! The tall recluse with the long beard!"

I was shocked. He knew a secret I kept to myself and related to no one, not even to him. It was then confirmed to me that the voice came from God Himself, and that the pope who is to come would indeed be Fr. Mena the Recluse.

I left him following my confession, after receiving his blessing and absolution. I then made my way to Cairo. There, unintentionally and without prior planning, I happened to meet Fr. Mena the Recluse's brother, Mr. Mikhail, at the Patriarchal Residence. Next to him was Azmy, the former pope's driver, who continued in service to Pope Kyrillos until his repose.

Upon getting introduced to [Mr. Mikhail], I told him, "Tell Fr. Mena, 'Congratulations on the patriarchate.'"

He was confused and perplexed about the matter, especially since the nomination committee had not yet convened. And Fr. Mena's name was never on people's mouths as much as the other names that were well-known at the time.

Mr. Mikhail and Azmy, the driver, both dismissed the idea, regarding what I said to be a kind of delusion; they sensed my strong inclination for a monk to be chosen as the pope. I confirmed to them that the matter was ordained by the Lord, and that this was His divine will. And I left.[42]

Fr. Mena the Recluse was indeed enthroned as Patriarch on Sunday, May 10, 1959, becoming Pope Kyrillos VI, and so the prophecy of Fr. Abdel Massih was fulfilled.

In the months following the enthronement, Pope Kyrillos received Fr. Luka in Cairo. He asked Fr. Luka about Fr. Abdel Massih and where he was currently living. It became clear to Fr. Luka that the Patriarch had longed to see Fr. Abdel Massih. The last time the two encountered one another was decades prior, in the wilderness, when the Pope was a young monk at the Monastery of Baramous.

---

42   The Arabic Life of Fr. Abdel Massih, 44–45.

The Enthronement of Pope Kyrillos VI
on Sunday, May 10, 1959

In 1962, Pope Kyrillos placed it in his heart to arrange a pastoral visit to the Diocese of Beni Suef and Bahnasa. He supervised the planning of the itinerary himself, explicitly ordering to include the village of Manahra in the schedule.

Metropolitan Mena adds, "No one knew the intention behind His Holiness' visit to Manahra, until later; he sought to meet Fr. Abdel Massih, to receive his blessings, and to request his prayers."[43]

The Pope entered the church and arrived at the door of the Sanctuary. Fr. Abdel Massih walked in a few moments later, proceeding down the aisle joyfully. Pope Kyrillos drew aside the veil of the altar and entered the Sanctuary to pray.

Metropolitan Athanasius[44] stood sternly at the Sanctuary door. Seeing the monk approach, he unexpectedly threw his arm in front of the door and barred him from taking another step.

In front of the entire congregation, he humiliated the monk, "[Being in] the countryside has made you blind!"

Fr. Abdel Massih withdrew, speechless, shrinking under the public rebuke. His face began to grow hot with both anger and embarrassment.

A string of uncomfortable threats followed, "And do not dare to enter the Sanctuary, otherwise the Pope will defrock

---

43   The Arabic Life of Fr. Abdel Massih, 42.

44   His Eminence Metropolitan Athanasius I (1883–1962) served as the fourth metropolitan of the Diocese of Beni Suef and Bahnasa, heading the very diocese Fr. Abdel Massih served in. He was ordained by Pope Kyrillos V in 1925 and fulfilled the role of the patriarchal Locum tenens, or Acting Patriarch, on two occasions: first, following the repose of Pope Macarius I from 1945 to 1946, and then again after the repose of Pope Yusab II from 1956 to 1959. He is particularly remembered for nominating Fr. Mena the Recluse to the patriarchate, after which he was ordained as Pope Kyrillos VI.

you from monasticism. You have not followed his decree, which orders all the monks to return to their monasteries."[45]

Fr. Abdel Massih, though deeply hurt, found himself steadfast. Ignoring the warnings of his metropolitan, he boldly marched into the Sanctuary to greet the Pope.

Pope Kyrillos concluded his prayers at the altar and turned around, finding the monk standing before him. What happened next stunned everyone present. The Pope, known far and wide for his holiness and spiritual stature, bent down and pulled this simple monk's hand towards him, kissing his hand several times. At long last, and after years of longing, he was finally receiving the blessings of Fr. Abdel Massih.

Those who observed the spectacle, including the metropolitan, were dumbfounded, their eyes widening in disbelief. Gasps could be heard spreading throughout the church. The holy Patriarch bends himself low and makes himself small before the monk with the tattered tunic!

Following the prayers, the Pope made his way out of the parish, his next stop being the city of Matai. With hundreds thronging him, his attempt to exit the church became increasingly difficult. The patriarch abruptly stopped

---

45   The Papal Decree of August 1960 ordered the return of all monks to their respective monasteries by September 30 of that same year. The decree was in part addressed to those assigned to serve outside the monastery, and more specifically to those who tarried in villages and their families' homes in order to evade the harsh living conditions of the desert. The dwindling numbers led to a dangerous decline in desert monastic communities. Having ascended the patriarchal throne, Pope Kyrillos VI commenced the efforts to better the living conditions of the monks and revitalize life in desert monasteries. With these improvements, the decree was issued to recall monks to the desert in order to rejuvenate monasticism. The consequence of disobeying or disregarding the papal decree was immediate defrocking.

walking. He turned and scanned the crowd around him, searching for a particular face amidst the people.

"Fr. Abdel Massih!" he called out, pulling aside the shawl on his head and motioning to him. "Please pray for me!"

The monk was deeply moved. He answered shyly, "Me pray for you, my brother? You have all of Christ with you!"

Bidding the Patriarch farewell, Fr. Abdel Massih found his feet taking him to the nearby Ibrahimiya Canal. Several people followed him, but he kept his distance from them all. He stood at the edge of the canal by himself. He was fuming.

He picked up a rock off the ground and began to speak crossly, "You, Athanasius, curse me in front of the people, and tell me the countryside has blinded me? I will knock you down to the ground!"

With that, he hurled the stone into the canal. Those who stood at a distance from him noticed what he did and assumed he was acting out of foolishness, as usual. However, at the same moment, over in the city of Matai, as Metropolitan Athanasius approached the city on foot, he was hit directly in the middle of his forehead with a stone. The source of the stone could not be traced.

And as he exited his vehicle and began making his way into the outer courtyard

Metropolitan Athanasius I,
Metropolitan of Beni Suef
and Bahnasa, (1883–1962)

of the church, he collided forcefully with a large tree, causing him to aggressively fall to the ground. Those nearby ran to him quickly and lifted him up. When the metropolitan recovered from the shock of the fall, Pope Kyrillos drew near to him and commented, "Fr. Abdel Massih did this to you."

Metropolitan Athanasius grew remorseful. He sought to ask the monk for his forgiveness, having wronged him. Mr. Mos'ad, the owner of al-Fida' newspaper, promptly made his way to Manahra, to the saint's cell, to bring him. Fr. Abdel Massih, on the other hand, apologized and refused to go along.

"It's nighttime," the monk remarked, "go tell him I forgive him."

Mr. Mos'ad returned to Metropolitan Athanasius and conveyed the message, which eased his conscience. Mos'ad, as witness to all of this, published his own firsthand accounts in his newspaper, detailing the entire incident.

Pope Kyrillos VI stands among parishioners at the church of St. Mary in Manahra. Fr. Abdel Massih was asked to stand next to the Patriarch for this photo, but he ran away like a madman. The people around the monk reprimanded him sternly, but the Pope intervened and defended him, "Leave him be! That man is a blessing."

The saint's biographer comments on the actions of Metropolitan Athanasius. He begins, "I believe that Metropolitan Athanasius is without justification..."

First, he was very familiar with the saint and was well aware of the extent of his spirituality. He also resided with him for a long time.

Second, the saint resided in Manahra as a solitary. As such, there was no Church canon which forces a solitary to abandon their solitary life, for he no longer shoulders any ecclesiastical responsibility. The solitary's connection with the Lord Christ is a direct one, which no one can intervene in, regardless of the circumstances.[46]

A Long-Awaited Child

Hanna Youaqim of Manahra, who was introduced earlier, emerges as a significant figure in the life of Fr. Abdel Massih, being the monk's steadfast companion and closest friend for a period of close to four decades. On one evening, Hanna extended an invitation to Fr. Abdel Massih to visit him.

As he entered the house, the monk settled himself comfortably on a woven floor mat, assuming his customary cross-legged position on the ground. The house was quiet, void of the sounds of children. Hanna and Mariam conceived and bore upwards of ten times, and each time Mariam would give birth, the child would die.

As they all conversed, in an abrupt turn of events, Fr. Abdel Massih, from the floor, suddenly burst out laughing.

---

46   The Arabic Life of Fr. Abdel Massih, 72.

And he could not control himself. He laughed until his stomach hurt. Hanna and Mariam were shocked by this completely unexpected outburst.

"What are you laughing at, Fr. Abdel Massih?!" Hanna asked.

Catching his breath, he finally managed to utter a prophecy through his gasps for air, "We're going to have a boy, and we will name him Makram. And in his baptism, we'll christen him Ajaybi."[47]

Hanna shook his head vigorously. Any faith he once had was long dead and buried with his children. "I don't want any more heartache, Father. Any child that comes dies."

Fr. Abdel Massih encouraged Hanna and his wife. With one hand resting on Hanna's shoulder, he began, "Do not be upset. By my Lady the Virgin, Makram will come. And I will live long enough to attend his wedding."

Indeed, shortly after the visit, Mariam became pregnant with a boy, carrying him to full term this time. She named him Makram and christened him Ajaybi. Fr. Abdel Massih lived to see this child grow up and get married.

After Makram's wedding, the monk once again found himself at Hanna's home. Mariam, gesturing toward the newlyweds, bid the monk, "Pray for Makram and his bride, so that God may bless them with good offspring."

His response sounded ridiculous, "Don't worry. Makram's wife will be dragging, and carrying, and bearing."

The family laughed off his answer, not grasping the significance of what he said. And yet, as time unfolded, his words proved prophetic indeed.

---

47   Literally, "the miraculous one."

Makram's wife bore three children, one after the other: the first and eldest, who was reportedly very stubborn, needed to be dragged by the hand, the middle child would be regularly carried on his mother's shoulder, and the youngest she bore within her womb, all simultaneously. Dragging, carrying, and bearing—all at once.

They will be Blessed

Metropolitan Mena writes:

> After my arrival in the village of Manahra, a member of our family, Mrs. Fawziya Hanna Girgis from Beni Mazar, when she heard that we are in the process of releasing the life of our saintly father, she explained that every single time she conceived, she would miscarry. She grew tired from all the medical treatment. So she met with our saintly Fr. Abdel Massih and asked him to pray for her.

> He told her, "Don't worry, you'll give birth to a boy and a girl! A boy and a girl! A boy and a girl! They will be blessed!"

> She explained that she was puzzled by his saying. Would she give birth to two children [or more]? Indeed, God granted her according to the prophecy of the saint—three boys and three girls; a boy followed by a girl, each time.[48]

---

48   The Arabic Life of Fr. Abdel Massih, 51.

The Palm Tree

In Manahra, there is a palm tree currently known as "Fr. Abdel Massih's Palm Tree." The story behind it, as recounted by all the residents of the village, is as follows:

Fr. Abdel Massih was sitting among a group of villagers, the oldest of whom was his closest friend, Hanna Youaqim. There was a small date tree nearby, no more than twenty inches tall, with about five leaves sprouting from it. Because the tree was so small, it had not yet borne fruit.

Hanna, in a playful attempt to amuse the monk, asked him, "Fr. Abdel Massih, what do you think? Will this palm tree bear red dates?"

The saint replied, contradicting him, "Yellow."

Then Hanna asked, "So, will it bear yellow dates?"

The saint responded, "Red."

This back-and-forth continued for a while, with each suggesting the opposite color. Finally, the saint affirmed, "It will bear both yellow and red."

The people present remembered his words, especially since no date tree bears dates with two colors.

Indeed, the palm tree annually bears dates that are half red and half yellow. It remains there to this day.

Your House is Going to Fall

Ebaid Yassa had just finished renovating his home, which neighbored the church of St. George in Samalut, in the eastern corner of the city. With the help of Moallem Farag Wassef al-Banna, Ebaid completely remodeled the house and painted it a bright white. Finishing the renovation efforts, he hosted Fr. Abdel Massih for two days.

As was his custom, Ebaid, before leaving the house to start the day, knocked on Fr. Abdel Massih's room door to receive his blessings. The monk opened the door and blessed him.

"Listen, Ebaid," Fr. Abdel Massih told him as he leaned on his walking stick, "make sure you take care of my bag when you move out and leave the house."

Ebaid was confused. He had just finished renovating the house! He responded, "Where would I go, Fr. Abdel Massih?"

"Didn't I tell you?" The monk began, "Your house is going to fall. Either way, you're free to do what you want."

He started to walk out of the house, leaving Ebaid unsettled and perplexed.

"I'm leaving," he waved casually as he walked into the street, "take care of my bag!"

The bag, which he left in his room, had nothing but a small book and a frayed shawl.

Ebaid followed him out of the house, calling out to him, frightened, "If the house falls, won't it collapse on the people in the street?!"

Fr. Abdel Massih turned around, "It won't fall on the street. It will collapse within itself, and only after midnight."

The monk nonchalantly continued walking, leaving Ebaid in a state of mounting panic. He ran back inside and described to his wife what Fr. Abdel Massih told him. Within the hour, he brought Moallem Farag, who oversaw the renovation project, to thoroughly inspect the house. The assessment concluded that the walls had developed a major structural defect, compromising the integrity of the entire building. Ebaid never told Farag about the words of Fr. Abdel Massih.

Ebaid vacated his house immediately and inhabited another. A mere five days after the last piece of furniture was moved out of his home, the frantic pounding of a local police guard, Mahmoud Seloufa, awoke Ebaid from his sleep at 3:00 a.m. The house had collapsed. And at the time the monk said it would happen.

Strangest of all, amidst the wreckage, only one room was left standing, completely untouched: the one Fr. Abdel Massih slept in. Mahmoud, still breathless from the run to Ebaid's home, testified, "That man must be one of the servants of God."

The Monk and the King of Egypt

One day, in July of 1952, Fr. Abdel Massih met again with Yacoub Bibawy, the well-known cotton merchant from Samalut. Fr. Abdel Massih entered Yacoub's house and found him sitting anxiously, and yet he did not relate to the monk what was distressing him.

Fr. Abdel Massih teased, "Yacoub, Farouk wants you. And he wants one of your cotton fields."

Yacoub struggled to hush Fr. Abdel Massih. The mere mention of the king's name could draw all ears to the walls of his house.

"Father," Yacoub glared, "stay quiet!"

"Don't be so worried," he smirked, "An officer will meet you. He will let you in through one door, and then out through another. And in two weeks, I will drive the big man out of the country for you. I'll send him to Italy! He'll go sell bread and falafel!"

Yacoub was terrified. King Farouk indeed had his eye on one of his fields and intended to seize the land without cause.

It seemed like the only possible solution was for the king to just—leave.

And, here, Fr. Abdel Massih testified that, in a fortnight, the Lord would make it happen.

The problem was, if someone happened to have heard this conversation, all trouble would come knocking at Yacoub's door. He was torn between believing and doubting. How could the king be expelled from Egypt?

From that day forward, Yacoub began observing whether or not the monk's riddles would prove true.

Precisely two weeks later—to the day—on July 23, 1952, the army carried out its revolution, overthrew King Farouk, and expelled him from the country for good, as was prophesied. The late Yacoub Bibawy never ceased telling all his loved ones about the prophecy of our saintly father, Fr. Abdel Massih.[49]

Spare Us, Lord

Metropolitan Mena remembers how in 1957, he was at the Monastery of the Virgin Mary in Jabal al-Tayr, Samalut, spending a retreat with Fr. Boutros Boutros and Fr. Boulos Boulos. These two priests recounted to him the following miracle, which he also verified with the villagers, the other priests, and the visitors of the monastery, all of whom remember it well.

---

49   The 1952 Egyptian Revolution, led by a group of nationalist military officers known as the Free Officers, marked the end of the monarchy under King Farouk I (1920–1965). Motivated by widespread corruption, inequality, and British influence, the Free Officers, including Gamal Abdel Nasser and Muhammad Naguib, orchestrated a coup d'état on July 23, 1952, causing Farouk to abdicate the throne, and establishing the Republic of Egypt. Farouk was exiled to Italy, where he would die at the age of 45.

One day, Fr. Abdel Massih was staying at the monastery. It was a quiet evening, and, as he sat silently, those with him saw him abruptly look up to the heavens and become completely disengaged.

"Your intercessions, O Virgin!" he began to scream, his eyes widening to an alarming degree.

The agitation of the people around him heightened the louder his voice became.

"Spare us, Lord!" he continued to shout, with his gaze still fixed on the sky. "Let it go to the cats and dogs!"

A few moments had passed before he fell silent again and looked back down. He turned his attention to those around him and smiled. They all stared at him; he had obviously gone mad.

The next morning, to the astonishment of all the monastery's inhabitants, every stray cat and dog on the monastery grounds was found dead, scattered all around. Not one was spared. The villagers realized that a plague had been imminent, ready to strike the region. Yet, at the word of the monk they assumed had gone insane, the Lord had lifted it from them.

I Want to Eat Fish

Fr. Abdel Massih sat one day on the shore of the Nile. Noticing him staring off into the horizon, a man standing nearby approached him.

"What are you sitting here for, Fr. Abdel Massih?" the man asked.

The monk promptly looked up at the man who was addressing him. Squinting from the sunlight, he answered, "I want to eat fish."

"You don't have a net or a fishing rod!" Presuming the monk to be speaking nonsense, the man left him alone.

Witnesses nearby saw Fr. Abdel Massih look back at the Nile and smile warmly. He pulled his cross from his chest pocket and extended his hand over the surface of the water, signing it with the sign of the cross.

Dozens of large fish instantly began to flock together below his hand, which was still outstretched, almost as if they anticipated being caught by him. Fr. Abdel Massih simply immersed his fingers in the Nile's cool water and pulled out only what was required for his next meal. Grasping the fish in his hands, he stood up and walked away from the shore. Witnesses nearby were unable to believe what they had just seen. They were astonished at the great authority God had granted this simple monk of great faith.

The Black Umbrella

The people of Manahra recall that when Fr. Abdel Massih was asked to pray for someone who was ill, and he agreed to go, the sickness would often leave at once. However, if the Lord revealed to Fr. Abdel Massih that this person would die, he would never enter their house and pray over them, no matter who the person was.

In the span of his over thirty-year ministry in Manahra, the monk never attended the death of someone sick; if the villagers, after seeking him to pray for someone, witnessed him prop his black umbrella on his shoulder and leave the village, it became known that the sick person would not survive.

For instance, a villager by the name of Tawfiq Saeed, who knew Fr. Abdel Massih well, had fallen seriously ill. One of Tawfiq's servants left the house to seek the monk's prayers for his master. He found Fr. Abdel Massih in a sugarcane field, standing alone in the middle of a few stalks.

Before the servant could approach, he saw the monk turn and speak; it looked as if he was addressing the air. Fr. Abdel Massih strictly adjured, "Don't come down now! Wait until I leave!"

Hearing these words, the servant realized that the monk was conversing with the angel assigned to take his master's soul. Still standing at a distance, he saw Fr. Abdel Massih place his black umbrella on his shoulder and make his way out of the village.

The servant hurried back to Tawfiq's house and reported to the family what he had witnessed and heard.

"You all know Fr. Abdel Massih and his ways," he said to them. "Master Tawfiq will not live to see another day."

Tawfiq passed away within the hour.

As was his custom, Fr. Abdel Massih did not return to Manahra until three days later, missing the actual death. As he usually did, he waited until the customary third-day prayers to return to the village and offer his condolences to the mourning family.

On the Brink of Death

Metropolitan Mena records that he visited the late Habib Stephanos before his passing and heard how his wife, Victoria, had fallen gravely ill. All her doctors had given up hope for her recovery. One day, Fr. Abdel Massih came to their home, and Habib saw it as the perfect opportunity for the monk to pray for his ailing wife.

Fr. Abdel Massih was led to the bedroom, where he found Victoria lying on the brink of death. The monk, feigning insanity, began to run around the bed three times.

"If you get better," the monk called out to her as he suddenly stopped in his tracks, "you'd better marry me."

Habib loved Fr. Abdel Massih and was well-acquainted with his strange ways. He smiled with hope, "Take her and marry her when she gets up. I've relinquished her to you."

Fr. Abdel Massih chuckled and then stood in silence for two minutes, gazing at Victoria. He quietly moved his lips in prayer and then touched her forehead with his right hand.

At last, the monk broke the silence and suggested, "Maybe an idea will come to you in two days to bring her to a doctor in Minya. He'll tell you she needs surgery, and he'll ask you to pay twelve pounds."

Habib, at once, took his wife to Minya for a medical evaluation. Following the exam, the physician confirmed, "She needs surgery." The procedure, he said, cost twelve pounds, no more, no less, just as the monk foretold. Strangely, following the simple preliminary examination, Victoria was miraculously healed.

Habib and his wife realized that Fr. Abdel Massih had advised them to see a doctor as a cover, to make it seem that the healing came through medical intervention, rather than through his hands.

Are You Going to Marry a Dead Woman?

An elderly woman by the name of Amelia Boutros from Manahra fell ill with a sickness that caused her family to await her death at any moment. Medical intervention had proved futile.

Upon hearing of Amelia's illness, Fr. Abdel Massih made his way to her house. He was taken to her bedside, where all her family members were gathered. They all stood around her, watching her take what they believed to be her final breaths. The room was flooded with a somber, gloomy silence, which was abruptly disturbed when Fr. Abdel Massih shouted, "I want to marry her!"

Amelia's son threw his hands up in the air in frustration. "Are you going to marry a dead woman? Is this a time to joke around, Father? She's dying!"

"But I want to marry her!" the monk was unyielding. "I swear by my Lady the Virgin, Amelia will not die. She'll get up and live many more years. My Lady is pure and chaste!"

Finishing his marriage proposal, Fr. Abdel Massih solemnly stretched out his hand, tracing the sign of the cross on her face. Drawing his hand back to himself, he announced, content, "I'm leaving."

As he headed to the door, he abruptly turned around and yelled, "Amelia! If you get up, would you agree to marry a black beggar like me?"

Amelia's son mockingly replied on his near-dead mother's behalf, glaring angrily at him, "When she wakes up, then by all means, marry her."

With a light-hearted laugh, Fr. Abdel Massih exited. The very moment Fr. Abdel Massih stepped out of the house, Amelia threw the covers off her body and arose, completely cured. It was as if she had just woken up from a deep sleep. Ululations and praises to God could be heard from down the street.

Make Some Space Next to You

The physician treating a young Younan Nashed of Manahra had been spending countless hours at the child's bedside, finally determining his symptoms to be those of bacterial meningitis.

"He only has a few hours," the doctor announced.

His family, therefore, began to prepare for his imminent death. His mother sat by his side, readying herself, at any moment, to let out her screams of lamentation. She then heard footsteps making their way into Younan's room. Looking up, she found Fr. Abdel Massih standing next to her, leaning on his stick. The monk was informed about the boy's looming death and quickly made his way over to "say his goodbyes."

"If your son wakes up," he winked, "will you marry me?"

She smiled and wiped her tears. Knowing this to be his typical jesting, she exhaled, "As soon as Younan rises, I'll marry you."

As usual, whenever anyone gave in to his ridiculous marriage proposal, he laughed and said nothing more. Then he continued towards the bed of the dying boy. Fr. Abdel Massih bent himself over the bed. He stretched himself out on the dying boy's feeble body, reminiscent of what the prophet Elijah did with the son of the widow at Zarephath.[50] Moments later, the monk used his arms to push himself up off the mattress, standing up once more.

Younan Nashed, who was on the verge of death

---

50   See 1 Kg 17:17–30.

"That's it," he breathed, already making his way out through the door. "He won't die. He will wake up."

The moment Fr. Abdel Massih left the home, Younan opened his eyes and jumped out of bed. It was as if he had never been ill in his life.

The Monk is a Cigarette Addict!

A young girl of eight years, Awatef, the daughter of Nader Samaan from Luxor, suddenly began to exhibit fits of shaking and loss of consciousness several times a day. Her father, having lost hope after many attempts to treat her, purportedly wished his daughter would die; it would surely be far better than living with such a condition for the rest of her life.

Nader had heard of a holy, wonderworking monk from Manahra. He also learned that the monk's disciple, Fr. Luka, would be stopping by their hometown before visiting his spiritual father. Determined to meet him, Nader brought his young daughter and waited for Fr. Luka to arrive.

When Fr. Luka came, Nader broke down in tears and begged him to take him and his sick eight-year-old child to Fr. Abdel Massih. Fr. Luka agreed to do so, and Hanna Youaqim came along with them.

When they reached the cell, Fr. Luka entreated Fr. Abdel Massih to pray for Awatef. He, on the other hand, pretended not to hear him. It was as if Fr. Luka said nothing.

Fr. Abdel Massih instead looked up to Hanna from the floor and asked him to give him a cigarette.

Hanna's face grew red; Fr. Abdel Massih made himself out to be a cigarette addict! He timidly pulled a cigarette from his pocket and extended it to Fr. Abdel Massih, who enflamed it immediately. He looked at it keenly, then put the burning side in his mouth, closing his lips over it. He began to blow the smoke outward instead of inhaling it in.

Awatef, at this point, was laughing uncontrollably; the monk clearly had no idea what he was doing.

"What's her name?" He asked, pulling the cigarette out of his mouth.

"Her name is Awatef," they answered in unison.

He turned to the child and stretched his hand out, the cigarette pinched between his fingers. "Take a puff from the cigarette, Awatef," he commanded, looking her directly in the eyes.

They all stood scandalized at his demand to the epileptic eight-year-old. The girl, still laughing, politely refused the monk's order.

And then, in a moment, Fr. Luka realized where this was going. He told her to obey him, take the cigarette, and put it in her mouth.

Awatef indeed submitted. She extended her tiny hand and took the cigarette from Fr. Abdel Massih. Still laughing, having never seen something so bizarre, she put the cigarette to her lips, with the lit end in her mouth.

"The girl is fine," he declared, watching her lips only touch the cigarette. "There is no disease in her. Now get up and get out of here."

Metropolitan Mena continues:

We were all shocked, and some of us believed that the Lord would work the miracle at the hands of the saint. And yet others [among us] doubted, believing that he had dismissed us in such a manner which, outwardly, seemed like a kind of folly.

And yet, in truth, [Awatef] was completely and immediately cured, and the matter was not revealed until after her travel. The disease never returned to her again, from 1958, even till the writing of these very words.

Her father visited us in Manahra on the sixteenth of July, 1977. I asked him about her. He responded that, since she placed the saint's cigarette in her mouth, she was completely healed, and the sickness never returned to her again. He also said she is married and has four children, and is in good health.

Here, it becomes clear to us that the saint foreknew the coming of the sick girl and prayed for her in advance, with assurance that she would receive healing. He then wished to conceal the ordeal by lighting a cigarette in our presence.

If there be offense taken by some [due to] the deeds of the saint, we shall address them; there was no offense found [in us] after the miracle had taken place. And a miracle was performed without a single doubt. Therefore, [his acts] are a work of self-denial and concealment. And as we have previously mentioned, what was said by one of the saints, "Virtue is like a treasure. If it is uncovered, it becomes robbed by vainglory."

As we have stated, not all of the fathers can act in such a way; rather, each has his own characteristic methods, whether they be in speech, behavior, or action. He takes this [upon himself], after much testing, till he has attained a high level of virtue. And what is important is the achievement of the goal itself, which he strives toward; silence may profit one, but not another. Knowledge may benefit one, but simplicity may be more advantageous to another. Therefore, each person endeavors to triumph over the self in the manner they find most suitable, and by the methods they can carry out with both precision and proficiency.

Am I the Second Christ?

Na'eema Hussein, a young Muslim woman from Manahra, had suffered from rickets since her childhood until she was nine years old, leaving her a paraplegic. Hanna Youaqim brought her to Fr. Abdel Massih at that time and asked him to pray for her.

Na'eema Hussein

He turned to Hanna and yelled, pretending to be insane, "So I am the second Christ? And they told you that I shine with light? I want to get married!"

Hanna persisted in begging him. The monk consistently refused and would not be convinced. Finally, Hanna adjured him by the Holy Virgin Mary, for whose love he was always singing.

When Fr. Abdel Massih heard the name of the Virgin, he laughed in joy, "Get up from here, girl!" She immediately rose and began to run.

Within moments of her taking her first steps, he strictly warned her, "If you tell anyone, you will return as you were."

The girl and her mother, however, overcome with joy, did not pay attention to his warning. Na'eema went about spreading the news everywhere, saying, "Fr. Abdel Massih healed me!"

Three days later, Fr. Abdel Massih met Na'eema. He glared at her and said, "Why did you disobey me? Go back and sit." She instantly became paralyzed again as before.

A few days later, he went to her home and stood at the threshold, saying to her, "Promise me that you will keep this secret and tell no one."

She made the promise, and after she vowed, Fr. Abdel Massih announced, "The Lord has healed you; rise from the ground."

She rose at once, whole and well. She kept her promise and did not tell anyone until after his departure.

Go Bring the Duck

While Metropolitan Mena walked through the streets of Manahra to visit someone ill, he was directed to the home of Labib Basilios Khalil.

The man accompanying the metropolitan on his visitations introduced the two to one another, "This is Labib, the one with the duck."

Metropolitan Mena raised an eyebrow, "What duck?"

"Hear it for yourself," came the reply. Then, turning to Labib, he said, "What's the story, Labib?"

He began telling how his family owned a fine male duck, carefully fed and fattened from the very start of the Great Fast. He had planned to slaughter it for the Feast of the Resurrection, and was eager to rejoice with his wife and children. But before the feast arrived, the duck suddenly died. For a family of limited means, the loss of the bird was devastating. Not long after, Fr. Abdel Massih passed by their home and saw Labib's wife crying bitterly.

He asked her, "What's the matter, woman?"

"The duck died, Father," she sobbed, "and I just threw it on the heap for the stray dogs to eat."

He ordered her, "Go bring the duck."

She repeated that it was dead, and she had discarded it. He insisted she retrieve the dead duck and bring it to him. She reluctantly arose from the ground, brought the carcass, and threw it at his feet.

Um Nabil Labib, who owned the duck

He raised his walking stick, gesturing to the canal in front of the house, "Go plunge it in the water."

He trailed closely behind, following her down to the canal as she clutched the dead duck by its legs. He stood over her shoulder, watching closely as she dipped it into the water.

"Push on it," he demanded, "until the water covers it completely."

Though she was confused, she surrendered. She kneeled and pushed; the carcass was now wholly submerged under the water.

"Push on it again," he ordered once more, this time directing her to keep it fully immersed for about five minutes.

"Now pull it out of the water and leave it here. Go get it some grass for it to eat."

Frustrated, she tossed the dead duck on the edge of the canal, "Father, it's dead!"

"I said go!" He yelled, "Bring it some grass!"

She got up and brought the grass as he had instructed. When she returned, she saw the soaking wet carcass begin to twitch. Within moments, it was running about, fluttering its wings. The Lord, seeing his love for those who were in need, gave Fr. Abdel Massih the power to bring the duck back to life. All of Manahra spoke of this miracle, surprised that a dead duck submerged under water for so long could possibly live.

Play with Us

There was an occasion when Fr. Abdel Massih was invited to a family gathering at the house of a man named Hanna Girgis in the town of Beni Mazar. After greeting everyone, the monk left the adults and joined the group of children in the house, all of whom ranged in age from seven to nine years old.

The elder sat cross-legged on the floor, just as they did, and began to join in their games. He encouraged them to repeat after him, "Say, 'the black beggar of a monk!'"

Nearby, a woman, referred to with the initials "T.L." overheard the children mimicking the monk. Before the monk's arrival, others around this woman had spoken so highly of him, attempting to persuade her of his holiness. She, however, scoffed; being influenced by the teachings of other denominations, she regarded all she was told to be fantasy. And as she heard the children shout the ridiculous words, her notions were confirmed.

In a whisper to those beside her, she gossiped in disdain, "What is all this you are saying about him? If this monk truly *was* holy, he wouldn't do this! Would a holy man do that?"

Although she ensured her whispers were inaudible to the monk, God revealed her words to him. Suddenly, she began to feel intense discomfort and swelling in her neck.

She screamed in agony, and those around her could not ease her pain. It was then that she began to realize that her disparagement of Fr. Abdel Massih had brought this affliction upon her. She quickly ran to him, collapsing at his feet and begging for his forgiveness.

"What's wrong with you?" he asked. "You could have come to play with us instead of murmuring. Children are loved by Christ!"

With this gentle yet firm rebuke, he encouraged her to seek innocence over appearances. And then, at the utterance of the words, "I forgive you," the swelling completely dissolved, and the pain ceased instantaneously. From that moment on, the woman held Fr. Abdel Massih in deep reverence and often sought his prayers and blessings.

He will not Pray the Liturgy

The late Fr. Youannis Kamal, priest of the church of the Archangels Michael and Gabriel in Giza, records that late one Friday afternoon, good tidings began to circulate in the village of Manahra, and the news eventually came to the door of Fr. Abdel Massih's cell. Bishop Athanasius II[51] was coming to pray the Raising of Evening Incense on Saturday evening, spend the night, and celebrate the Divine Liturgy the following morning.

---

51 At the time of his visit, he was not elevated to the rank of Metropolitan.

Several people, upon receiving the news, promptly made their way to Fr. Abdel Massih. He welcomed them into his cell, and they surrounded him, some sitting at his feet.

"Our father, the bishop, is coming to spend the night and pray the Liturgy, Father," they related to him.

"Yes, yes," he began, "he will come, but he will not pray the Liturgy."

Those in the cell did not know whether to believe him or not; he regularly mingled reality with foolishness. After all, the bishop himself personally telephoned the mayor and told him his plans.

On Saturday, the car carrying the bishop arrived to Manahra. Villagers surrounded the vehicle carrying palm branches, leading their bishop to the church of St. Mary with joy. Bishop Athanasius prayed the Prayer of Thanksgiving and began the service of Vespers.

In the middle of the service, a car sent all the way from Cairo arrived at the church. The driver exited his vehicle, entered the church, and hurriedly approached Bishop Athanasius.

"Your uncle has departed, Your Grace," the driver broke the news, whispering into his ear. "The Patriarchate sent you a car to take you to Cairo tonight. The funeral is tomorrow morning at 10:30 at the church of St. Peter and St. Paul in al-Abbasiya."

Having concluded the services, Bishop Athanasius delivered a brief announcement, apologizing for the unexpected itinerary change; he would neither be able to spend the night nor celebrate the Liturgy with them in the morning. He quickly made his way out of the church and was driven directly to Cairo.

Fr. Abdel Massih secluded himself in his cell for the entire day. Congregants immediately left the church and knocked frenziedly at his door.

He called out from within, without opening, "He raised incense and left, didn't he?"

"Exactly, Father!"

"My mother told me," he replied. "She said he would come, but would not sleep over or pray the Liturgy."

His "mother," he later divulged after much pressure, was the Holy Virgin Mary.

The situation was later related to the bishop. Even after years passed, Bishop Athanasius would chuckle and reminisce, "He will come, but will not pray," whenever someone brought up Fr. Abdel Massih in conversation before him.[52]

Bishop Athanasius II said, "Before I visited Manahra again, he had departed to heaven, and so I missed the blessing of meeting him."[53]

Bishop Athanasius II
of Beni Suef (1923–2000)

---

52   Hegumen Youannis Kamal, *Qiddīsīn Taẓāharū bi-al-Gunūn* [Saints who Feigned Madness]. (2006), 40–41.

53   The Arabic Life of Fr. Abdel Massih, 17.

Chapter Six

Married on the Day of the Feast

Sunday, April 7, 1963

The Feast of Lord's Entry to Jerusalem.

Palm Sunday.

Fr. Abdel Massih had just completed the Divine Liturgy at the church of St. Mary. It was noticed that an unusual sense of joy overtook him in the middle of the Liturgy.

He stood at the door of the church and greeted the people walking out, grabbing their hands and extending a bizarre invitation to them, "You're all invited! I'll be crowned and married on the day of the feast."

Fr. Abdel Massih insisted that each commit to memory the date of his wedding, which was to be officiated at the church on the Feast of the Resurrection in a week.

"Don't forget! It's on the day of the feast! Come and attend the wedding, you're all invited."

The responses were, most of the time, dismissive. A mere, "Sure, Father."

Some silently assumed him to be rambling, as usual. Others, sarcastically curious, inquired about the identity of the supposed bride. Still, there were those who feared he had finally lost his mind.

He would repeat the same declaration persistently throughout the week of Holy Pascha. He walked around the village, often going from door to door, inviting more wedding guests.

Tuesday, April 9

Two dear acquaintances of the monk had come to visit him: Sheikh Eleia Ayad, the village leader of Kom al-Arab in Matai, and Fanous Youssef, an onion merchant from the city of Maghagha. Accompanying the two was Hanna Youaqim.

Standing outside, each of the monk's guests vied to host him at their house for a meal on the Feast of the Resurrection. He, however, answered them nothing but the same phrase.

"I'll be crowned and married on the day of the feast."

Eleia nudged the monk and laughed, "It seems like you're going to die on the day of the feast, Father."

Fr. Abdel Massih rested his arm on his stick and responded with a smirk, "So now you're prophesying, Sheikh Eleia?"

Fanous, on the other hand, was completely unsettled. He interjected, "What are you saying, Eleia? God forbid, Father. May you live a long life."

Fr. Abdel Massih turned to Fanous and urged him not to distress. "Don't upset yourself, my brother! Don't be upset!"

With a single, deliberate strike, the monk drove the tip of his walking stick into the soft soil beneath his feet. He hollowed out a hole in the dirt, expanding it gradually.

"Here's a hole," the monk remarked.

Another strike of the stick into the soil followed. Breaking up the earth, he dug a second hole beside the one he just made.

"And here's another hole," he mumbled again, looking pointedly at Fanous.

Fanous looked up from both holes and gasped, "Perhaps *I'll* be the one who dies!"

Fr. Abdel Massih smiled, not saying another word. He then changed the subject, continuing to repeat the phrase,

"I'll be crowned and married on the day of the feast."

Saturday, April 13.

Bright Saturday.

Fanous Youssef unexpectedly departs to Paradise, to the shock of his family and acquaintances. The monk's prophecy was fulfilled.

Fr. Abdel Massih prays the Divine Liturgy for the Feast of the Resurrection that evening, concluding the service a little after midnight. Howling reminders to the congregation about his wedding, he excitedly runs back to his cell and locks the door behind him.

He is getting married in the morning.

Sunday, April 14, 1963

Parmoute 6, 1679 AM.

The Glorious Feast of the Resurrection.

A few young men stop by the monk's hermitage to wish him happy returns for the feast. They knock on his door, and yet it seems he is not there. There is no answer.

They leave the cell and begin searching for Fr. Abdel Massih; he must have woken up early and gone into the village. With Manahra being so small, the entire village was combed within an hour. There was no trace of Fr. Abdel Massih. No one had seen him since the previous night.

The visitors return to the cell and knock again, this time bringing the mayor with them. No answer came from within. Fearing the worst, the door is broken down.

Fr. Abdel Massih, who lived his life evading praise, willingly choosing the derision of men over honor, was found stretched out on the dirt floor, with his arms crossed over his chest, having surrendered his soul into the hands of the Lord after a struggle on earth spanning seventy-one years. His face was seen to be emitting light, described as looking like the face of an angel.

The monk's words, absurd as they sounded, proved true, as usual. He was indeed crowned on the Feast of the Resurrection; crowns of chastity, patience, and struggle now adorned his head.

His desire to be married is now finally realized: he rejoices with Christ the true Bridegroom, in the holy bridal chamber, the Paradise of Joy.

The men carried the monk's pure body to the church, chanting the hymn of joy and victory, "Christ is Risen!"

Word quickly spread that the monk widely believed to be insane had departed. Many of those who supposed so stood in the funeral procession—his wedding procession—stunned and in disbelief. Would the man who foreknew the precise day and time of his repose a week in advance truly be insane? In fact, those who recklessly gave themselves over to judging him—these are the irrational ones!

"We called him crazy, we called him stupid," they whispered to one another as they walked behind the casket, "it seems we are the ones who are crazy and stupid!"

Fr. Abdel Massih was interred in a mausoleum in the cemeteries of Samalut, on the grounds of the Monastery of the Virgin Mary in Jabal al-Tayr. His relics were later moved to a reliquary in a church bearing his name in Manahra.

One of the only two photographs ever taken of Fr. Abdel Massih of the Monastery of St. Macarius. Here, he poses for a photograph, after much pressure, with his closest friend, Hanna Youaqim on Friday, August 25, 1959, on the porch of Hanna's home in Manahra.

The Life of Metropolitan Mena
Metropolitan of the Diocese of Girga, Bahjurah and Farshout

Introduction

The life of Metropolitan Mena became the embodiment of the difficult harmony between the call to public ministry and the desire for solitude. So great was his love for the desert that, at the height of his service in the episcopate, he asked to be relieved of its responsibilities. He became the metropolitan who willingly left his throne and became a solitary, though it was only for a time. Even after returning to his diocese, beneath the weight of his episcopal vestments was an ascetic of uncommon stature. In his solitude, he had grown profoundly intimate with God.

Upon him were bestowed the spiritual gifts associated with the desert fathers; he prayed with the Spirit-borne anchorites, and even became chief among them. His association with the anchorites was widely attested to, so much so that, on one occasion, the students of the Theological Seminary asked Bishop Shenouda, the General Bishop of Christian Education and dean of the seminary (later Pope Shenouda III), about who the anchorites were. His response was deliberately brief, so as to not reveal too much, "Abba Mena, the metropolitan of Girga, will be able to speak to you on this subject."[54]

---

54   Magdy Kyrillos Grant, *Al-Qalb al-Baseer: Ayam Modee'a fi Hayat Muthalath al-Rahamat Niyafat al-Anba Mena Mutran Girga: Hayah - Mungazat - Fadd'el – Mo'gizat* [The Discerning Heart: Illuminated Days in the Life of the Thrice-Blessed Metropolitan Mena of Girga, His Life, Achievements, Virtues, and Miracles]. (The Diocese of Girga, Bahjurah, and Farshout. February, 2004], 166. [Henceforth, the Arabic Life of Metropolitan Mena].

His discipleship to Fr. Abdel Massih of the Monastery of St. Macarius grafted him into the lineage of the great fathers of Coptic monasticism. It was Metropolitan Mena who brought Fr. Abdel Massih to the knowledge of the wider Church. Now, however, the time has come to turn our gaze toward the hierarch himself: a man who stood at the intersection of being present with the people, yet bearing within himself the stillness of the wilderness.

CHAPTER ONE

Childhood and Upbringing

Qozman Ishak Sarapamon was born on Friday, May 9, 1919, in the village of Rahmaniya Qibly, Nag Hammadi, to a modest farmer family, the second oldest of five children. His father Ishak owned a small plot of fertile soil, which he plowed and planted diligently. His mother Melouk dedicated her life to her husband and children, and cared for nothing other than her salvation and that of her household.

Qozman Ishak Sarapamon

As a child, Qozman woke up at dawn to till the land with his father. At dusk, after his father returned home, he would stay behind for a few more hours, finding his father's land a suitable place to pursue contemplation. Amid this expanse of soil, Qozman cultivated an inclination for seclusion.

Still a young boy, at dawn of every Sunday, Qozman saddled his father's donkey and rode to the Monastery of St. Abba Palamon[55] in the village of al-Qasr, praying the psalms on the road. He usually made his way to the monastery on Saturday evening and spent the entire night praying the Midnight Praises. He concluded his weekly retreat with the Divine Liturgy the following morning.

On the feast of Abba Palamon, Qozman's family had a tradition of carrying prepared meals and bread to offer to the pilgrims at the monastery gates, many of whom came from great distances to celebrate. They also did this during Holy Week, giving special attention to the strangers and the poor.

Every Sunday at the monastery, Qozman would find a simple monk officiating the Liturgy. He came to know that this monk, named Fr. Boulos, received his tonsure at the Monastery of St. Macarius, but was pursuing the solitary life in a mountain cave in the desert nearby. Because of his widespread piety and asceticism, Fr. Boulos was given the name "the Worshipper," and with his increasing interactions with Qozman, he took him as his disciple.

Qozman's visits to the cave of Fr. Boulos the Worshipper eventually became an almost daily occurrence, and the two became inseparable. He sat at the feet of this solitary and began to find that he longed to live as Fr. Boulos lived.

---

55   Abba Palamon the Anchorite (ca. 315 AD) lived in solitude in a mountain cave in what is now known as the village of al-Qasr near Nag Hammadi. He is the spiritual father of Abba Pachomius the Great, and therefore an exemplar of pre-cenobitic Egyptian monasticism. He is known only through *The Life of Pachomius*, which records that it was under his guidance that Pachomius received his foundational spiritual formation before founding the cenobitic system. Abba Palamon is commemorated annually on the 25th day of the Coptic month of Epep, which corresponds to August 1st. His monastery, which lies less than one mile from the village of Rahmaniya Qibly, was at one point filled with monks. It is now a place repeatedly used for gatherings by the Spirit-borne anchorites.

CHAPTER TWO

Running to Scetis

One of Qozman's relatives, Mesak Youssef, had a particular bearing on him. Though he exceeded the age of ninety, Mesak was a regular pilgrim to the desert monasteries, specifically that of St. Anthony the Great in the Eastern Wilderness. Whenever Mesak returned from his trips, Qozman would sit with him, and, with great attentiveness and eagerness, he would hear him relate what he saw. He met the holiest of monks, the most righteous ascetics, even the Spirit-Borne anchorites, whenever God allowed him to encounter them.

Metropolitan Mena, himself, recalls:

[He] used to tell me many stories about the anchorite fathers. Because of this, my heart was kindled with divine love to the point that I would stand praying for long hours, and I often longed to see these anchorites myself. And this is what happened:

Before my monasticism, I took residence in a room in Nag Hammadi. One day, one of the anchorites appeared in my room. He stayed with me for a whole day and spoke to me about the greatness and works of God. He then spent the night with me. Before leaving the next morning, he said to me,

"One day, you will become like us."[56]

In the morning, I bid him farewell and stood at the door watching him as he went away. He walked a short distance, then disappeared from my sight, and I could no longer see him.[57]

Qozman became assured, after developing an overpowering love for the Lord, that he was called to continue his journey on earth as a monk. He decided that he must leave for the monastery. He was barely fifteen years old. He devised a plan with a childhood friend, Matta Youhanna, that they would secretly flee to the monastery together. The only one with knowledge of their intention was a mutual friend of theirs, Toma Behnam.[58]

Indeed, in 1934, the two went to Farshout and boarded a train there. They purposely avoided the train station of Nag Hammadi, where they could be easily recognized. From there, they fled to the dependency of the Monastery of St. Anthony in the village of Boush, and their families grew more anxious with each passing day because of their sudden disappearance.

When they arrived at the dependency, Qozman and Matta were immediately turned away. They were told they were too young to become monks and were ordered to return home. They received instruction to take this period of their lives to examine themselves and discern whether or not their desire was sincere.

---

56   Meaning, he would attain the spiritual stature that would make him worthy of the anchoritic life.

57   *Al-Anba Mena al-Sa'eh wa-l-Aba' al-Sowah* [Abba Mena the Anchorite and the Anchorite Fathers] by Children of Abba Mena, published under the auspices of the Diocese of Girga, Bahjurah, and Farshut, 11.

58   Later Hagumen Azer Behnam.

Qozman was disappointed. He returned home, only to be received by the callous reprimand of his father. However, there was no power on earth, he believed, that would prevent him from pursuing monasticism and trying again.

In 1936, two years later, he attempted to escape once more, this time on his own, to the dependency of the Monastery of St. Anthony. Qozman was on the verge of finally being accepted into the monastery, especially due to his firm determination. His father, Ishak, however, discovered his whereabouts. Once more, Qozman was compelled to leave.

This was followed by another attempt at fleeing in 1938. Qozman was, again, returned by his father, who believed that monasticism is a path trodden solely by the poor and unsuccessful.

His Purity

The desire remained in Qozman's heart, regardless of where he was. He was adamant on living the three vows of monasticism—voluntary poverty, obedience, and chastity—even if he dwelt outside the walls of a monastery.

As a young man, he once traveled to Cairo and boarded a tram for public transportation. On one of these rides, he found himself surrounded on all sides by young women; the tram was so crowded that there was no room to move. Fearing that temptation may take root in his heart, and that he would inadvertently come into contact with the passengers around him, he chose to leap from the window of the tram while it was still in motion.

He recounted, "I was going to die. But I told myself it would be better to die than to fall into sin."[59]

---

59   The Arabic Life of Metropolitan Mena, 17.

And yet, the Lord saved him. Though this was an extreme act, and not one to be imitated, his action was rooted in the seriousness with which he viewed sin. Sin, in his eyes, was not something to be reasoned with, nor was it to be approached lightly. It is a power to be fled from entirely.

Leaving the World

In 1939, Qozman decided that the time had come. Nothing could prevent him any longer. He left the world and travelled to the Monastery of St. Anthony, recalling the stories he heard from his aunt's husband. He remained at the monastery for one year, after which he left. He found it too comfortable for himself.

Fr. Boulos the Worshipper had told him stories of the monastery of his repentance,[60] which was in a completely debilitated state, where there were monks practicing the strictest means of asceticism. Qozman took to the Wilderness of Scetis, knocking on the door of the monastery he was told so much about: the Monastery of St. Macarius.

Hegumen Fr. Maximus of St. Macarius, the abbot at the time, tried to discourage him. He told him that the path was hard, that he was still young, and that he would not survive there. Yet he did not relent, not for a moment.

Fr. Maximus then took him by the hand and led him to the *tafos*[61]. Together, the two stood before an empty burial vault. Pointing to the dark and ominous tomb, Fr. Maximus exhaled, "You want to stay? This is your cell. Make yourself at home." With great eagerness, he replied that he would gladly do so.

---

60   That is, the monastery where a monk originally receives his tonsure.

61   The Greek τάφος (transliterated as "tafos"), literally, "tomb," is the term still utilized in the monasteries of Egypt when speaking of the designated area wherein reposed monastics are buried.

He indeed inhabited the empty tomb, as menacing as it appeared, and made it his cell. He later described that it was in this tomb that he experienced firsthand the presence of the Lord Jesus Christ, who came to him, blessed him, encouraged him, and strengthened him.

Fr. Maximus, seeing Qozman's resolve, later assigned him a simple cell, like the rest of the novices.

Weeks passed, and Qozman received a letter from his father, Ishak. Tearing the envelope open, he read, "I will no longer dispute the will of God. You were my son. Now, you are my father. Pray for me, your mother, and your siblings."

Matta Youhanna came to visit his lifelong friend. He yearned to join him.

"Your path is in the world, Matta," Qozman smiled, "protect yourself there, and that shall be enough for you."

The monks of the monastery assigned Qozman the daily obedience of baking the oblation bread for the Divine Liturgy. He mastered the craft, to the point that he excelled above those who spent decades doing the job.

His obedience to the elders was without limits. The assembly of monks loved him, and so, on the morning of Sunday, April 30, 1939, he was tonsured a monk at the age of nineteen years old. He was given the name Luka of the Monastery of St. Macarius.

Shortly after his tonsure, he took a walk with some of his fellow monks and was drawn to the chapel in their path. He heard absolutely beautiful voices chanting in the church. The monks with him confirmed that they heard nothing; only he was able to clearly hear the prayers.

At his first step inside the church, Fr. Luka witnessed a vast number of anchorites filling the chapel, joining one another in prayer. He attended with them. They welcomed him silently into their midst but did not speak a word to him.[62]

He was ordained a priest a few months after his twentieth birthday, on the morning of Saturday, November 18, 1939. In 1943, he was elevated to hegumen and became economos[63] of the monastery.

Fr. Luka of St. Macarius

---

62   *Al-Anba Mena al-Sa'eh wa-l-Aba' al-Sowah* [Abba Mena the Anchorite and the Anchorite Fathers] by Children of Abba Mena, published under the auspices of the Diocese of Girga, Bahjurah, and Farshut, 41

63   The Economos (Arabic: *al-Wakīl)* is a monastic who is administratively responsible for the affairs of the monastery. He reports to the abbot, who is spiritually responsible.

CHAPTER THREE

Experiences in the Monastic Life

The Missing Loaf

One night, Fr. Luka was baking the loaves of Qorban. There was an opening in the roof of Bethlehem[64] that allowed for the smoke coming from the oven to escape. After completing the long and exhausting labor, he placed the loaves into the oven. When the time came to remove the tray, he froze; one loaf had vanished from the batch. It had inexplicably gone missing.

Fr. Luka's mind raced. His confusion quickly gave way to irritation. He counted the loaves again, then again. The result was the same. One was gone. How could one of the loaves he diligently produced under the weight of heat, dehydration, and drowsiness, simply disappear?

His thoughts then turned to the monks. Had someone slipped into Bethlehem under the cover of darkness to play some sick practical joke? Was he now expected to grind more wheat, knead fresh dough, shape and stamp another loaf, wait for it to rise, and bake all over again—all for a single missing loaf?

---

64   The room where the Qorban is baked bears the traditional name "Bethlehem," tying the city of the Lord's Nativity to the place where the bread that becomes His Body is baked.

In a fit of frustration, Fr. Luka turned around and loudly admonished the unseen prankster with his priestly authority, "There is no absolution or forgiveness for he who took the loaf!"

Before his eyes, an illumined man instantly descended through the opening in the ceiling and stood before him in Bethlehem. He had an unkempt and lengthy white beard. He was clothed in a tattered monastic habit. He held the missing loaf in his hand.

In a tranquil and hushed voice, the man timidly bowed his head, "I have sinned, absolve me."

Frightened, Fr. Luka instantly replied with the proper priestly response, "May God absolve you. Absolve me!"

"I took the loaf, Father," the elder confessed.

"Who are you?"

"We are a group of anchorites in need of the Qorban to celebrate the Liturgy together."

The Spirit-borne anchorite, having received the instantaneous absolution, immediately disappeared before Fr. Luka's eyes, taking the loaf with him.

Fr. Luka was terrified. He ran out of Bethlehem and came across the first elder in his path, and explained what had just taken place. The elder laughed and simply instructed him not to count the loaves of Qorban again.

The Three Holy Elders

At the direction of the elders at the monastery, he sought for himself a father confessor at the Monastery of Baramous, an elder named Fr. Philotheos. Fr. Luka saddled the monastery's donkey and made the journey to Baramous once a month for confession.

On the way, he would routinely stop at the neighboring Monastery of St. Pishoy and the Monastery of the Syrians to take the blessings of the fathers, and, often, to spend the night.

Once, in 1945, while traveling to Baramous for confession, he decided to rest overnight at the Monastery of St. Pishoy. He chose an elevated, level patch of ground beside the cell of Fr. Ezekiel of St. Pishoy and lay there to sleep.

In the middle of the night, he was awakened by a voice, saying, "Get up. There are jewels beneath you." He fell back asleep, but the voice came again. He ignored it a second time. When the voice spoke a third time, he not only heard it but felt someone push his hand, causing him to rise immediately. He found no one there.

He then brought a shovel and began to dig beneath the spot where he had been sleeping. There, he uncovered the relics of three desert fathers from the early centuries of monasticism. Desiring to take a small portion of the relics—such as a strand of hair or a fragment of bone—as a blessing, he sought and received permission from Fr. Girgis Abu Kaffa, the economos of the Monastery of the Syrians. He then carefully removed a portion from each body, wrapped them in a handkerchief, and returned to his monastery, where he placed the relics beneath the veil covering the tomb of the Forty-Nine Martyrs.[65]

---

65   The Forty-Nine Martyrs of Scetis are a group of monks from the Monastery of St. Macarius who were massacred by the Berbers during their third raid on the wilderness in AD 444. The envoy of Emperor Theodosius the Less and his young son were also martyred with them. Refusing to go into hiding, they all welcomed martyrdom and willingly chose to witness to Christ and be brutally killed at the hands of the Berbers. They are commemorated yearly on the 26th of the month of Tobe, coinciding with the third of February.

He was curious about who these three holy elders were. And so, Fr. Luka fasted, without food or drink, for three days. On the third day, they appeared to him in glory and splendor, introducing themselves and revealing their names.[66]

The saints instructed Fr. Luka to return what he had taken in the handkerchief to the Monastery of St. Pishoy. He went to his abbot, Hegumen Matthias Hanna of St. Macarius,[67] and asked for permission to return the relics. Fr. Matthias refused and told him that he would take care of the matter himself. Instead of granting permission to travel to St. Pishoy's, Fr. Luka was informed that he had been chosen to begin studies at the Monastic Theological College in Helwan and was to depart immediately.

After the discovery of the bodies, the monks wished to prepare reliquaries and transfer the relics to the ancient church so that the monks and novices could receive their blessing. Suddenly, an unusual swarm of gnats filled the monastery, as though the saints themselves did not wish for their bodies to be publicly venerated. They desired to remain hidden. The relics were therefore buried in the *tafos*. At the very moment the door was sealed, the gnats vanished.

---

66   In an audio-recorded interview featured on a cassette entitled, "*The Man of Humility*," released by the Monastery of Archangel Michael in Girga, Metropolitan Mina recounts how the saints introduced themselves as monks bearing the names of Basil, Gregory, and Cyril. They also conveyed that they are mentioned daily during the Midnight Praises. He clarified, however, that these monks said they died as martyrs for their faith in Christ, and therefore cannot be the authors of the three Divine Liturgies (those of St. Basil of Caesarea, St. Gregory of Nazianzus, and St. Cyril of Alexandria). Therefore, he said, the resemblance in names is purely coincidental.

67   Metropolitan Mikhail of Assiut (1920–2014).

Fr. Luka in his early days of monasticism

Service in Esna

After graduating from the Monastic Theological College on May 30, 1950, Fr. Luka was assigned to serve in the city of Esna. Two days later, on June 1, 1950, he departed for Esna and took up residence at the Monastery of St. Mettaos on Mount Asfoun.[68] Alongside restoring and renovating the monastery that became his home, Fr. Luka began an active ministry among the many surrounding villages.

A young Helmy Aziz, who lived in a small village near Esna, later recalled:

> I was a young boy, only eleven years old, and it was the first time I ever saw a monk…. And because of the difficulty of transportation, it was sometimes necessary [for Fr. Luka] to spend the night in the village after sunset. On one such time, he spent the night in our village, and in our house in particular. After dinner, everyone gathered around him to hear his sweet words, which were filled with grace. It was a night I will never forget; Fr. Luka spoke to us about the holy monks, those who dwell in the deserts, and about their biographies, their austerity, their struggles, and their miracles. We listened to him with

---

68   Abba Mettaos (Matthew) al-Fakhūry was an Egyptian desert father of the eighth century AD. He was tonsured a monk in one of the Pachomian monasteries and later embraced the life of solitude in a cave nearby. Mettaos took upon himself the handiwork of pottery, which he inherited from his father, and became known by the epithet *al-Fakhūry* ("the Potter"). Though he was appointed abbot of the Monastery of Asfoun, he, in deep humility, often referred to himself as "Matthew the Poor." He was renowned for his spiritual gifts, which included healing the sick, exorcising demons, clairvoyance, and even raising the dead. He attained such holiness that wild animals would be tamed in his presence, approaching him without fear to eat from his hands. His departure is commemorated annually on the seventh of Koiahk (coinciding with the sixteenth of December).

deep longing. And I do not exaggerate when I say that the person of Fr. Luka, and his captivating stories about the monks, is what subconsciously placed in my heart the very first seed of monasticism.[69]

It happened that during his time of service in Esna, one of the anchorites appeared to Fr. Luka. The anchorite held his hand and suddenly, in the blink of an eye, Fr. Luka found himself in the Monastery of the Martyrs in Akhmim[70] [which is roughly 190 miles distant from Esna].

The monastery had not yet been renovated. As such, it was uninhabited, and the area around it was unpopulated. He found an entire congregation of anchorites waiting for him in the ancient church. He celebrated the Divine Liturgy for them since none of them was ordained a priest. After distributing the Holy Mysteries to all of them, he was taken back to Esna as quickly as he left it.[71]

---

69   Fourteen years after that gathering, Helmy would join the Monastery of the Syrians and be tonsured as Fr. Paphnutius of the Syrians. He would eventually be ordained as its abbot on June 6, 1993, becoming His Grace Bishop Mettaos.

70   The Martyrs of Akhmim are a vast multitude of Christians slain in the Upper Egyptian city of Akhmim (ancient Panopolis) during the Diocletianic persecutions in AD 302. The massacre occurred over a period of three days, beginning on the eve of the 29th of Koiahk and continuing through the first of Tobe. It claimed the lives of approximately 8,140 martyrs, including men, women, and children, becoming one of the bloodiest episodes of the Diocletian persecution, and a defining moment in the Coptic Orthodox Church's martyrological tradition. The site of their martyrdom later became the Monastery of the Martyrs (*Dayr al-Shuhadāʾ*), located east of modern Akhmim near al-Hawawish. The relics of these fourth century martyrs, many found to be still bleeding and incorrupt to this day, are buried in and around the monastery.

71   *Al-Anba Mena al-Saʾeh wa-l-Abaʾ al-Sowah* [Abba Mena the Anchorite and the Anchorite Fathers] by Children of Abba Mena, published under the auspices of the Diocese of Girga, Bahjurah, and Farshut, 12.

Fr. Luka was granted the gift of exorcism while in Esna. Hundreds of people, Christians and Muslims, came to him seeking healing. When he sensed that the church in Esna was turned into a hospital for the sick and demoniacs, feeling that his ministry had taken a blow, he pleaded with the Lord, in tears, that this gift may be lifted from him. He requested this to continue on his spiritual journey unimpeded, fulfilling his daily spiritual rule in full faithfulness. Indeed, God took away the gift of exorcism from Fr. Luka.

Build My Church!

After spending nearly a year restoring the Monastery of St. Mettaos, Fr. Luka was reassigned to serve at the church of the Holy Virgin Mary in Esna. He took a small brick room in the churchyard as his cell. The ancient church, dating back to the third century, was in a lamentable state. Its walls were crumbling, and it was left to decay because of neglect.

One night, as Fr. Luka sat alone in his cell, a light suddenly filled the room. From within that brilliant light emerged the Blessed Mother of God. She stood before Fr. Luka with sorrow in her eyes. Her garments were torn.

Fr. Luka was startled and distressed. He asked, "Why are your clothes torn, my Mother?"

She answered softly, "Because my church is in ruins. You are a monk serving my church—but my church is in ruins! Get up and build my church, lest it collapse!"

The Blessed Mother then assured him that she would remove every difficulty and obstacle that he would encounter. Without delay, Fr. Luka gathered the faithful and the youth of the church and began the work of reconstruction. He labored with the builders and carried bricks and sacks of cement upon his own back. By 1955, his efforts blossomed into a cathedral that still stands to this day.

*The church of the Holy Virgin Mary in Esna, renovated by
Fr. Luka of the Monastery of St. Macarius in 1955*

Fr. Abdel Massih of Manahra:
A Guide and Father Confessor

In 1955, when Fr. Luka received word of the repose of Fr. Philotheos of Baramous, he knew he needed another spiritual guide. He began to pray fervently for the Lord's direction. Around this time, he met Hanna Youaqim of Manahra, who told him that Fr. Abdel Massih of the Monastery of St. Macarius was living as a solitary near his home in Manahra.

Although Fr. Abdel Massih belonged to the same monastery as he did, the two had never lived there at the same time. Fr. Abdel Massih had spent years wandering between monasteries long before Fr. Luka even joined.

They had crossed paths only once before, in 1950, in Helwan, while Fr. Luka was in his fifth year at the Theological College. He longed to see him. To his surprise, Fr. Abdel Massih appeared before him in Helwan, smiling, "Didn't you want to see me? I have come to you!"

They sat together for three hours, after which Fr. Luka walked him to the train station and bid him farewell. This was the only time he met him, and since then, he left a lasting impression on his soul.

"Do you think," Fr. Luka asked Hanna, "he would agree for me to visit him?"

Hanna replied with the affirmative. At once, they made their way to Manahra. The two met again, and Fr. Abdel Massih immediately began hearing his confessions.

Fr. Luka traveled to Manahra each month for confession, and on every visit, he found Fr. Abdel Massih waiting for him along the road, though he had never once informed him of the time he would arrive. And although the people perceived in Fr Abdel Massih a deliberate guise of insanity, whenever he administered the Sacrament of Confession, he revealed himself to be remarkably precise, profoundly loving, deeply spiritual, and exceedingly firm.

And in comparing Fr. Abdel Massih as a father confessor with his previous confessor, the late Hegumen Philotheos, Fr. Luka would consistently say, to the end of his life, "There is no one who has attained the level of Fr. Abdel Massih."

The Fruit of Obedience

On one occasion, Fr. Abdel Massih sought to test Fr. Luka's obedience. It was a Wednesday, and when the time for the midday meal arrived, he brought out a chicken that one of his spiritual children had prepared for him. When Fr. Luka gently reminded him that the day was a fasting day, Fr. Abdel Massih replied by reminding him of the virtue of obedience.

And so they ate together. Only afterward did it become evident that the chicken was spoiled, so much so that the animal that had been given the chicken's innards died shortly after consuming them. However, no harm befell the two fathers.

At that moment, Fr. Abdel Massih turned to him and said, "Such is the fruit of obedience. God grants authority to His children to taste the most lethal poison, and yet it will not harm them."[72]

Leaving Esna and Settling in Cairo

One night, as Fr. Luka was alone in his cell within the church, he heard a knock at the door. When he opened it, he found a woman standing before him at the doorstep.

"What is it?" he asked her.

With disturbing boldness, she tempted him to sin with her.

Fr. Luka recoiled. "What you are doing is a sin," he rebuked her. "Shame on you! In any case, I will take your coming to me as if you came to confess, not to sin. Bow your head. I will pray the absolution over you—but never return to this again."

---

72   The Arabic Life of Metropolitan Mena, 127

The woman broke into tears. Fr. Luka read the prayer of absolution for her, and she departed, having repented. That very night, Fr. Luka sat down and wrote to his abbot at the Monastery of St. Macarius.

"Summon me back without delay," he wrote. "I must return to my monastery."

He did this so that his departure from the church, coming by command of his abbot, would raise no questions among the people. Shortly thereafter, he left and returned to the Monastery of St. Macarius.

The return was brief. He was soon summoned back into the world; his growing reputation reached Metropolitan Mettaos of Sharqiya (1910–1975), who assigned him to serve in the small village of Monshaat Ghaly Mansour.

Once, when he went to Manahra, Fr. Luka said with longing, "Fr. Abdel Massih, I want to live with you and be discipled by you. That is my only wish!"

Fr. Abdel Massih laughed. "I am a beggar! As for you, the day will come when you hold a cross in your hand, wear a cross on your chest, and extend it for the people to kiss."

Hanna Youaqim's wife, Mariam, sat on the couch opposite them. She commented confidently, "Fr. Luka, it seems you will become a metropolitan."

Metropolitan Mena remembers:

After the ordination of St. Pope Kyrillos VI on May 10, 1959, I visited my saintly father in Manahra [to interpret] a vision I saw. When I arrived, I mentioned nothing concerning the vision.

After about an hour, he told me, "Get up and go to Cairo. Maybe our brother and father will keep you with him there."

Nothing was on my mind except to confess and to receive an interpretation for the vision I saw. And what was strange was that, before I left, he interpreted it to me without my mentioning it to him!

I arose, per his command, and travelled to Cairo, and I entered the patriarchate and found a new display: I saw people entering, and others leaving. I saw groups and individuals in a way that was unprecedented. I asked about this new phenomenon, and it was told to me that Pope Kyrillos opens his door to everyone, and that he offers his blessing to all his children. He also listens to all their complaints himself.

I went in, just as one of those entering to receive his blessing only. When he saw me, he said, "Come, Fr. Luka! Where have you been? And how is Fr. Abdel Massih?"

I told him, "I am [currently] in Monshaat Ghaly, in Sharqiya, Your Holiness. And Fr. Abdel Massih is still in his place in the village of Manahra. I was with him just twenty-four hours ago."

He asked me to take a seat, but I refrained [from doing so]. He ordered me a second time, so I obeyed [his request] timidly.

After a moment, I asked His Holiness' permission to depart, but he told me, "Go, get your things, and come from the village you are [staying] in."

I sat silent. He said a second time, "I told you to go get your things and come!"

I replied, "As you say, I will obey, Your Holiness." I never mentioned to him anything about what our saintly father [Abdel Massih] said!

I departed, being accompanied by the well-wishes of His Holiness, though I was confused about the entire matter. However, I fulfilled [his order] and brought my things. He then ordered to give me a room in the Patriarchal Residence.[73]

And so, following Fr. Abdel Massih's initial prophecy, Fr. Luka was summoned away from his service of villages and appointed as a live-in secretary to Pope Kyrillos VI.

---

73   The Arabic Life of Fr. Abdel Massih, 46–47.

Becoming Metropolitan of Girga

Girga in Shambles

After Girga's Metropolitan Yusab became the Pope of Alexandria on May 26, 1946, the diocese would be without a shepherd for fourteen years.[74] And although the Patriarch often delegated several bishops to visit Girga every so often, he was forced to set aside his attention to the diocese in order to deal with the responsibilities of the Church at large. Girga soon found itself effectively unsupervised, and much of the diocesan authority fell into the hands of wealthy laymen and landowners.

With the repose of Pope Yusab II, and the enthronement of his successor Pope Kyrillos VI, discussions began as to who would be ordained as the next Bishop of the Diocese of Girga, Bahjurah, and Farshout. But the selection of a candidate became a point of bitter contention. The nominee proposed by Pope Kyrillos was rejected by the people, and the nominee proposed by the people was refused by the Pope. The entire process devolved into quarrels, tension, and open strife. There was no consensus, and no peace, among the people.

Metropolitan Mena recalls:

---

74   Canon law forbids the enthronement of another bishop or metropolitan over a diocese so long as its original shepherd is alive.

About six months after the ordination of the Pope, a friend came to me. He was working as a teacher in Esna during the days when I served as the priest for the church of the Virgin there. He was later transferred to Girga, and he informed me that he had assembled with the people in Girga… concerning the ordination of a metropolitan for it.

One of those present [at the meeting] stood up and said, "My brothers who are present, I have a suggestion. Let us put all disagreements aside. Let us cast away both the nominee of His Holiness the Pope and our nominee. And let us begin searching for a person other than these two candidates."

"And after a back-and-forth discussion," [my friend told me], "your name was presented to those in attendance, and it was met with approval. So I came to inform you."

When I heard these words from him, I feared. If the Pope finds out, he will certainly suppose that I sought to nominate myself behind his back! In truth, and the Lord is witness, there was no desire in me toward this grave rank.

When I heard from my friend what occurred in Girga, I arose at once and made my way to Manahra, where my saintly father resided. I presented the matter to him in his capacity as my father confessor and my spiritual guide.

I was astonished when I heard the reply from him, "Go, tell the Pope, 'Ordain me metropolitan.'"

I told him, "I do not desire this position, and I know its danger to myself! Also, how can I ask the Pope for such an unusual and unpraiseworthy request, something unheard of in monasticism? Can a young girl bluntly order her father, 'Marry me off! I want to get married?' It is inappropriate for me to say to the Pope, 'Ordain me metropolitan!' And at the same time, I have no desire whatsoever for this position!"

He replied, "I told you."

I went out from him in the utmost confusion; I was caught between my aversion to the position, my sense of the gravity of the responsibility, and the prospect of disobeying my saintly father.

Finally, for the sake of obedience, I travelled to Alexandria. There, I was astonished to hear the Pope say to me, "Congratulations! You have no absolution or forgiveness if you forbid anyone from helping you or nominating you."

I smiled in a way that hinted there was something I was concealing about the matter. His Holiness, may God benefit us by his prayers, began, "Where were you? Who were you with? What did he tell you?"

My tongue ceased from speaking. I thought to myself, "Is the Pope saying this as a casual remark? Or did it slip into his mind that I met with someone from Girga? Or perhaps God revealed to him what took place between my saintly father and me! Was there some kind of wireless link between them?"

"So?" He finally said, "You're silent."

I therefore felt compelled to tell him frankly what the saint said to me, "He told me to tell Your Holiness, 'Ordain me a metropolitan!'"

He laughed a laugh from which one could sense that their spirits were joined. And he responded to me, "After Fr. Abdel Massih—may his prayers be with us!—told you these words, and gave you this command, and he is a great and saintly man, one of the anchorites, do you want to disobey and run away? Do not dare disobey or flee, lest the fish swallow you, as it did Jonah."

At this point, he—may the Lord grant repose to his soul in the Paradise of Joy—said to me with these exact words: "Listen, my son. I know that you are not inclined toward high positions. But your acceptance of this particular diocese at this time, and I say this frankly, is a service to me personally. I dismissed the [previous] nominee for Girga, and the Lord will surely appoint him elsewhere. They refused my candidate, and so I want you to accept your ordination over Girga.

"I know very well that you will face many hardships there, but the Lord will be with you through the prayers of our father Abdel Massih. And I will always remember you in my prayers, that the Lord may make your path prosper."

He repeated to me, "Do not disobey Fr. Abdel Massih or me, for he is a great saint, and I know him well." Then he said, "Put your trust in the Lord."[75]

Upon hearing these words, Fr. Luka was filled with peace. His conscience was eased. Knowing that Pope Kyrillos promised to pray for him personally was a source of great comfort to him. However, the matter was kept private between the two of them; Fr. Luka's name was not suggested to the committee in Girga again.

---

75   The Arabic Life of Fr. Abdel Massih, 47–49.

The prominent leaders in Girga narrowed down and decided on the names of several nominees. Each of their names would be written on a separate piece of paper and placed on the altar of the church of Archangel Michael in Girga. On Sunday, June 23, 1960, the Divine Liturgy would be prayed. At its conclusion, an altar lot would be cast. A child would be blindfolded and led to draw a single piece of paper, and the monk whose name is chosen would become the next bishop of Girga. The papers included the names of the following candidates:

1. Hegumen Antonios of the Monastery of the Syrians[76]

2. Hegumen Matta al-Meskeen[77]

3. Hegumen Angelos of the Muharraq Monastery[78]

4. Hegumen Timotheos of the Monastery of St. Macarius[79]

A blank piece of paper was also placed among the names. If selected at the altar lot, it would be understood that God did not favor any of the candidates.

On the night of the altar lot, Fr. Timotheos telephoned Pope Kyrillos. He excused himself from being included among the nominees. The Pope attempted to persuade him to accept his nomination, but Fr. Timotheos was unyielding and would not be convinced.

Pope Kyrillos, in turn, contacted the diocese headquarters in Girga and ordered, "Write the name, 'Hegumen Luka of the Monastery of St. Macarius,' my secretary, in place of Fr. Timotheos' name."

---

76   Pope Shenouda III (1923–2012).

77   The spiritual father of the Monastery of St. Macarius (1919–2006).

78   Metropolitan Maximus of al-Qalyubiya, Shobra al-Khayma, and Quesna (1911–1992).

79   Bishop Timotheos, the General Bishop (1918–1999).

القرعة الهيكلية

تقـــــــديم

مطــــرانا للابروشــــيه

بعد أن نشاور أراخنة أبروشية جرجا للابارِكين يتقدموهم السيد لوجيهه الاستاذ صابر مشرق بروح المحبة .

وبعد أن استعرض المجتمعون عدة أسماء من الآباء الرهبان المشهود لهم بالعلم والتقوى والحزم . استقر الرأى بالاجماع على اختيار الآباء الرهبان الآتية أسماؤهم : ـ

١ ـ قداسة القمص متى المسكين وهو وكيل بطريركية الاسكندرية سابقاً ـ راهب جامعى تقى واعظ

٢ ـ قداسة القمص انطونيوس جيد . ليسانس آداب ودبلوم معهد التربية العالى ودبلوم الكلية الاكليريكية ومدير عبلة مدارس الأحد ـ تقى واعظ

٣ ـ قداسة القمص انجيلوس المحرقى أمين مكتبة البطريركية وكان مرشحاً للبطريركية ـ تقى ورع ثقافته دينية

٤ ـ قداسة القمص بيمو تأوس المقارى و وكيل مطرانية أسيوط تقى مثقف ثقافة دينية

• ـ ورقة بيضاء لا تحمل إسماً

وبعد انتهاء قداس صباح الأحد ٢١ يونيه بكنيسة الملاك بمدينة جرجا يقوم جناب الآب القمص جرجس عبد المسيح راعى الكنيسة باستدعاء شماس طفل لسحب ورقة القرعة التى تسفر عن اختيار الروح القدس ويعلنها قداسة الآب الراعى على الصليبين ؟

A pamphlet detailing the altar lot and its candidates,
which was distributed to the faithful in Girga

After the celebration of the Divine Liturgy, the altar lot was carried out. To the surprise of all, a name unknown to the entire congregation was drawn and displayed to them: Hegumen Luka of the Monastery of St. Macarius.

The matter was already appointed by God. Long before the list of candidates was finalized, long before the altar lot was even considered, God had chosen Fr. Luka to shepherd Girga, and He revealed this to both Pope Kyrillos and Fr. Abdel Massih.

However, none of those in attendance at the altar lot were made aware of the sudden change in names ordered by the Pope. Because of this, Girga's lay leaders collectively developed an almost immediate ill feeling for Pope Kyrillos and the monk he was about to ordain.

Ordination to the Episcopate

On the morning of Sunday, August 7, 1960, which coincided with the first day of the Fast of the Holy Virgin St. Mary, the Divine Liturgy commenced. Following the reading of the Acts of the Apostles, held by the arms according to tradition,[80] Fr. Luka was led into the Cathedral of St. Mark in Azbakiya and stood before the altar. Pope Kyrillos, with ten senior members of the Holy Synod, laid their hands on Fr. Luka, and the Pope announced, "We call you, Abba Mena, a metropolitan over the Diocese of Girga, Bahjurah, and Farshout."

He was raised to the rank of metropolitan, not a mere bishop, per the prophecy of Fr. Abdel Massih. And the name choice, it seems, was an indication as to how much the Pope loved him; he was given the name of Pope Kyrillos' own intercessor.

---

80   It was common for a monk, out of humility and a sense of deep unworthiness, to flee from his ordination as a bishop or patriarch. Church history records instances where nominees, chosen against their will, were led into the church forcefully held by the arms to prevent their escape. In some situations, chains were reportedly used.

Fr. Luka's modest cap was traded in for a turban. His simple black cassock was now concealed under golden vestments. He received an ivory-tipped pastoral staff from the hands of the Patriarch, and with it many prayers and good wishes, for a very challenging ministry lies ahead.

The ordination of Metropolitan Mena
on Sunday, August 7, 1960

Receiving his pastoral staff and vestments
from the hands of Pope Kyrillos VI

On the appointed day, Metropolitan Mena was escorted to the train station. The Patriarchate had reserved a car to carry him and a few bishops to Girga for the enthronement rites. But as the train began to move, so did the thoughts and anxieties within him. The faster it made its way down the tracks, the faster his mind raced. What awaits him in Girga?

The train slowed to make a surprising, unscheduled stop at the Matai Train Station. Metropolitan Mena spotted a familiar, tanned and wrinkled face out the window; he saw Fr. Abdel Massih eagerly clutching at his stick, watching the train come to a halt. All of the metropolitan's anxieties suddenly vanished, and he stood up instantly to greet him.

As he boarded the car, Fr. Abdel Massih hurried forward and covered his spiritual son's hands and cheeks with kisses. Metropolitan Mena gestured toward the seat and said, "Come, sit beside me, Fr. Abdel Massih!"

"No," he replied. He lowered himself to the floor of the aisle instead.

Without hesitation, the newly ordained metropolitan left his seat with the other bishops, and sat down beside him on the floor. He accompanied him on the train all the way to Minya.

Metropolitan Mena evokes to memory the counsel he gave him from the floor of the moving train:

He gave me advice that I will never forget, which was, word for word: "Beware of pride, for it shall cause the Spirit of God to abandon you. Imitate your Master, who says, 'learn from Me, for I am gentle and lowly in heart, and you will find rest for your souls.'"[81]

----

81   Mt. 11:29.

Then he said to me, as His Holiness the Pope had said, with only a slight difference in expression, "Fear not, and be strong in the face of the tribulations you will encounter. Let not your faith weaken, nor allow your resolve to falter. In doing so, you will perceive that the hand of the Lord is with you."[82]

As for his first spiritual father, Fr. Boulos the Worshipper, he came to the episcopal residence in Girga to congratulate him; he spent the night there. The next morning, Metropolitan Mena urged him to remain and dwell with him in the residence. He promised to provide him with all the simple needs of the cave. Yet Fr. Boulos respectfully declined. He told him that he favored, instead, the solitude of the mountain over a life confined within the walls of the episcopal residence.

Fr. Boulos the Worshipper

Tribulations

Arriving at the church with the convoy of bishops, Metropolitan Mena was greeted with an almost immediate sign of hostility.

---

82   The Arabic Life of Fr. Abdel Massih, 49.

"These bell patterns," they commented as they listened closely, "are ones of mourning!"

Some of the townsfolk, in protest to the Pope and the new metropolitan, manipulated the bellringer of the church of Archangel Michael to strike the bells with the traditional, interrupted bell pattern used to announce news of death or the start of a funeral. A group of people, including a few Muslims, ran into the bell tower and put a stop to the sorrowful bell tolls. The enthronement rites were prayed without further incident, but the air was thick with opposition.

One man in particular harbored an intense hatred for Metropolitan Mena. He knocked on his neighbors' doors and pressed them to avoid going to welcome the new metropolitan. And while Metropolitan Mena personally invited the man to several celebrations and events, encouraging amiability, he insisted on enmity. Metropolitan Mena would later label him, "Alexander the coppersmith."[83]

This man had a routine of sending horrible letters, brashly handwritten and signed, to Metropolitan Mena. One day, he sent a letter with contents so vile that the metropolitan, crumbling the letter, angrily yelled, "May the Lord make your blood boil like you made my blood boil!"

The man was struck with leukemia and died shortly after.[84]

⸙

Metropolitan Mena continued to serve and continued to love, even if the love was unrequited.

---

83   St. Paul writes in his second epistle to Timothy, "Alexander the coppersmith did me much harm, may the Lord repay him according to his works" (2 Tim. 4:14).

84   The Arabic Life of Metropolitan Mena, 48

At the beginning of his ministry, he traveled to Bahjurah, intending to visit one of the town's well-known figures. This man was known to have a deep dislike for the metropolitan, and yet, despite hearing of this, Metropolitan Mena was resolved to visit him all the same.

Seeing the metropolitan enter his house, the man scoffed, "Why did you come? Get out!"

The metropolitan calmly submitted and turned around to walk out of the room. "I'll leave your house," he sighed, "but I'll be back in fifteen days."

He left and immediately returned to Girga. Fifteen days later, the man suddenly died. His family came asking Metropolitan Mena to travel back to Bahjurah and preside over the funeral. And though he could have easily delegated any priest to preside, especially due to the disrespect he received from the deceased, not to mention the long journey, he agreed immediately.

Upon entering the church, he walked up to the casket, gently knocked on the casket's cover, and whispered tenderly, "I forgive you. I forgive you. I forgive you."[85]

Fr. Raphael Abba Mena, the disciple of Pope Kyrillos VI, recalls, saying:

I personally saw him when he used to go to Pope Kyrillos VI. Sometimes, once a month, other times every six months, and sometimes every three months. He became very, very close to His Holiness Pope Kyrillos. Of course, he would ask him about everything, great and small. I think Pope Kyrillos was among those who encouraged him to be patient,

---

85   Ibid., 54

steady, loving, and well-loved with the troublesome people; Pope Kyrillos himself was like that. As such, Metropolitan Mena grew close to him, and [the Pope] would guide him with these same counsels. Naturally, he became like him.

Resignation and Withdrawal
to the Solitary Life

The life of solitude became a sincerely profound desire in the heart of Metropolitan Mena, and it spanned his entire life as a monk. Since his days sitting at the feet of Fr. Boulos the Worshipper in the cave, and throughout his time in discipleship under Fr. Abdel Massih, he yearned to be like them, to live the full measure of the monastic life.

In 1977, having tendered a letter of resignation as metropolitan of the diocese, he received the following reply from His Holiness Pope Shenouda III. The reply is indeed precious and invaluable; in it, the Patriarch quotes directly from Metropolitan Mena's own letter, which puts into words the innermost longings of his heart:

Your Eminence, Metropolitan Mena:

Peace and grace from the Lord, whom we entreat to guard you as a precious vessel, in which His holy and blessed will be fulfilled at all times, and even beyond.

We have received your letter, dated June 2, 1977. In it, you indicate that you consider your priestly ministry like that of Martha, and that you yearn for the good portion of Mary, by sitting at the feet of Christ in a life of stillness.

You have given examples of bishops who have left their sees for the life of solitude, like Mar Isaac [the Syrian], St. Ammonius, St. Paphnutius, and St. Gregory of Nazianzus, [the latter of these] told a bishop who was a friend of his, "Leave the thrones to those who love them and seek after them. As for you, be like me." You mention in your letter that you cherish and revere these words.

You say after, "Since I no longer consider myself responsible for shepherding the people of my diocese, I leave the matter to Your Holiness to act in wisdom, and as the Spirit of the Lord directs you."

You also mention that this desire of yours is "an irrevocable will."

You urge me in your letter, "I implore Your Holiness, by the name of the Lord Christ, by His holy Body and precious Blood, by the Blessed Theotokos, by the angels, martyrs, and saints, and by St. Abba Pishoy, that you leave me to live in the peace of solitude. I ask that you consider me as no longer existing in this life; my wish, and the delight of my heart, is to be cast into the sea of forgetfulness, forgotten by all mankind."

I have read the copy of your letter, which you delivered to the metropolitans and bishops, bidding them all, in Christ Jesus, to support and aid you in spending the rest of the days of your sojourn on earth in the peace of solitude.

I have also read your announcement, published in al-Ahram newspaper, which states the same.

Thus, for the above reasons, I find myself incapable of standing against your holy desire and your unwavering will. Hence, I declare to you that your desire is hereby accepted.

Effective immediately, you are relieved of all pastoral obligations in the Diocese of Girga, Bahjurah, and Farshout.

I pray that the Lord God may grant you the blessings of solitude and stillness. May He keep the wars of the demons far from you. May He confirm you on this path, as had occurred with Mar Isaac, St. Paphnutius, and St. Ammonius. I will send you several spiritual and ascetical books, which will help you on this path.

I have delegated Their Graces, Bishop Youannis, the Secretary of the Holy Synod and Bishop of al-Gharbiya; Bishop Pishoy, Bishop of Damietta, al-Barrary and Kafr al-Sheikh; and Bishop Paphnutius, Bishop of Samalut; to deliver this letter to you.

Be safe in the Lord. May the Lord be with you and preserve your life in His love.

Pope Shenouda III

June 18, 1977

رسالة قداسة البابا إلى نيافة الأنبا مينا

صاحب النيافة الأنبا مينــا

سلام ونعمة من الرب ، طالباً منه أن يحفظكم آنية يعمل فيها إرادته المقدسة ، كل حين ، وبعــد ...

تسلمنا خطابكم المؤرخ ١٩٧٧/٦/٢ الذى تقولون فيه إنكم تحبون خدمتكم الكهنوتية كخدمة مريثا ، وانكم تختارون النصيب الصالح الذى لمريم بالجلوس فى حياة الهدوء، عند قدمى المسيح ، وتضربون أمثلة لأساقفة تركوا كراسيهم إلى حياة الوحدة مثل مار اسحق ، والقديس أمونيوس ، والأنبا يغنوتيوس ، والقديس أغريغوريوس النيازينزى الذى تعتزون بقوله لأحد أصدقائه الأساقفة «فاترك أنت الكرسى لمن يحبونها، وكن مثلى » . وتقول فى خطابكم إنك تسرّ بهذا القول وتقدسه . وتقول بعد ذلك « إنى إذ أعتبر نفسى غير مسئول عن رعاية شعب إيبارشيتى ، أترك لنيافتكم الأمر للتصرف بحكمة وكما يملى عليكم روح الرب » . كما تقولون إن هذه « إرادة لا عدول فيها » .

وأنتم لى فى خطابكم « أناشدكم باسم السيد المسيح ، وجسده ودمه ، وبالقديسة والدة الإله وبالملائكة وبالشهداء وبالقديسين ، وبالقديس الأنبا يسطوى أن تتركونى أنا أعيش فى هدوء الوحدة ، وأن تعتبرونى غير موجود على قيد الحياة ، فإن أمنيتى ومسرة قلبى أن أطرح فى بحر النسيان من البشر جميعاً » .

ولقد قرأت نسخة من خطاباتكم التى أرسلتموها إلى الآباء المطارنة والأساقفة ::اشدوتهم فيها فى المسيح بسوع أن يعاندركم ويساعدركم على قضاء بقية أيام غربتكم على الأرض فى هدوء الوحدة ، وترفقون نسخة من خطابكم لى ...

كما قرأت إعلانكم الذى نشرتموه فى جريدة الأهرام بنفس المعنى .

أرى نفسى غير مستطيع أن أقف ضد رغبتكم الروحية المقدسة ، وإرادتكم التى لا عدول فيها ، وأعان لكم قبولى لهذه الرغبة وعدم مسئوليتكم منــذ الآن عن ايبارشية جرجا وبهجورة وأرمنط . وأصلى إلى الله أن يعطيكم بركة حياة الوحدة والهدوء ، ويبعد عنكم حروب الشياطين ، ويثبتكم فى هذا الطريق الروحى كما حدث لمار اسحق والأنبا بينوده والأنبا أمونيوس . وسأرسل لكم بعض الكتب الروحية والنسكية التى تعينكم فى هذا الطريق .

وقد كلفت أصحاب النيافة الأنبا بولس سكرتير المجمع المقدس وأسقف التربية ، والأنبا يسطوى أسقف دمياط والبرارى وكفر الشيخ ، والأنبا يغنوتيوس أسقف سمالوط ، يحمل هذه الرسالة إليكم

كونوا سالمين فى الرب . الرب معكم يحفظ حياتكم فى حبه .

١٩٧٧/٦/١٨ البابا شنوده الثالث

The original letter by Pope Shenouda III, published by the Pope in al-Kiraza Magazine, in which he grants permission to Metropolitan Mena to begin pursuing the solitary life

He had his eye on the very place his dear spiritual father resided in, that is, Manahra. He revealed his desire to Metropolitan Athanasius II of Beni Suef (1923–2000), who was pastorally responsible for the village.

Metropolitan Athanasius approved joyously, "The entire diocese is at your disposal! As of this day, you are Metropolitan of Manahra!"

The two drove to the nearest church, and a meeting was called with the clergy of the surrounding region.

"From this day forward," Metropolitan Athanasius ordered, "[consider] Metropolitan Mena [to be] Metropolitan Athanasius while he is in Manahra. He is your metropolitan; he is not a guest. He has come to take the blessings of his spiritual father, Fr. Abdel Massih. And just as we took the blessings of Fr. Abdel Massih here, we will be taking the blessings of Metropolitan Mena as he comes for solitude and worship."

It was even ordered that Metropolitan Mena be mentioned in the liturgical Litany of the Fathers, directly after the name of Pope Shenouda III.

There were disputes as to where the metropolitan would live; many offered to move out of their own homes and leave them to him. He, however, thanked them all and committed to living in a small room within the church adjacent to Fr. Abdel Massih's cell.

One may question the reason for Metropolitan Mena's resolution to leave his diocese, insinuating an apparent escape from pastoral obligation or an attempt to flee from difficulty in the ministry. In reality, he was not fleeing labor; he was returning to the labor he knew best. He had accepted the episcopal office out of submission to Christ and His Church, and he sought release from it with precisely the same spirit. The desert had never loosened its hold on him.

Metropolitan Mena with Metropolitan Athanasius II of Beni Suef

He also affirmed later that this holy desire had a goal: the revealing of the sanctity and the honor due to God's chosen vessel, Fr. Abdel Massih of Manahra.[86] And so, at his first step in Manahra, he set out to begin making this holy desire of his into reality.

He began gathering stories, memories, precise dates, and miracles attributed to Fr. Abdel Massih. For over two years, he compiled first-hand accounts and sought out hundreds of eyewitnesses to the saintly man, visiting their homes and inviting them to his own quarters.

In 1979, he released his book, *Seerit Qidees Mo'aser: al-Qis Abdel Massih al-Maqari* [The Life of a Contemporary Saint: Fr. Abdel Massih of the Monastery of St. Macarius], which, as he described, would have been impossible to write amidst his responsibilities, and he needed to be dedicated to this task.

Returning the Body of Fr. Abdel Massih

During his time as a recluse, another holy wish began to surface. His Eminence remembers:

> I began to be urged strongly by the thought of transferring the body of Fr. Abdel Massih of Manahra from the cemeteries of Samalut, and this inner prompting continued to preoccupy me day and night.
>
> I sought the will of God in the Divine Liturgy and in prayer, and I found myself at peace regarding this. As such, I began preparing a large coffin made of white musk wood into which we would transfer the body of Fr. Abdel Massih.

---

86   See the Arabic Life of Metropolitan Mena, 68

Then, [I commissioned] another coffin, adorned and lined with velvet on the inside, and decorated with Formica on the outside. After, I obtained a Permit for Transfer of Human Remains [to relocate him] from the cemetery of Samalut to Matai.

All of this I did after I became certain that Fr. Abdel Massih wanted to be moved from his resting place; he was buried in a grave that was not fitting for him, and the Lord wanted to make him manifest.[87]

After the preparations, I told Mayor William, "I want to bring the body of Fr. Abdel Massih here."

The mayor replied, "Tomorrow we will bring him!"

Early the next morning, at dawn, the mayor's wife heard three powerful knocks on the door. The mayor's carriage driver, whose name was Saleeb,[88] was standing beside the carriage.

When the mayor's wife opened [the door], she found no one at the door.

She called out to Saleeb, "Who knocked at the door?"

---

87   In a video interview titled *A Talk of Memories*, produced by the Monastery of Archangel Michael in East Girga, Metropolitan Mena relates that Fr. Abdel Massih began appearing to him daily throughout the period in which he sought to discern the will of God concerning the relocation of the saint's body. These continual appearances left no doubt in his heart that Fr. Abdel Massih himself blessed and approved the transfer.

88   This Saleeb is the deacon who lived contemporaneously with Fr. Abdel Massih and who, together with the late Hegumen Youhanna Suleiman, priest of the church of the Holy Virgin in Manahra, witnessed Fr. Abdel Massih's hands shining with rays of light at nine in the morning.

Saleeb answered, "No one! There was no one here!"

Everyone immediately understood that Fr. Abdel Massih himself was in a hurry regarding this matter; he was the one who knocked on the door because he wanted to awaken the mayor so that he could complete the task.

The mayor and his men descended to the bank of the Nile River, carrying the empty coffin that had been prepared. There was no wind for them to take the boat to the eastern bank.

The mayor whispered, "Please, Fr. Abdel Massih, we need your help."

And immediately the wind blew, and the boat carried them to the eastern bank.

They went to the cemeteries of Samalut at Jabal al-Tayr, carrying the new white coffin. They pretended that they were repairing the door of the tomb, so as to avoid drawing attention to themselves. And so, they opened the tomb. Then they removed the coffin containing the body of Fr. Abdel Massih. They placed the coffin within the other coffin and then returned with it to Manahra, rejoicing.[89]

I Want to be Your Neighbor

The last holy wish during the period of solitude, as described by Metropolitan Mena, was as follows.

There was a plot of land directly adjacent to the cell of Fr. Abdel Massih. The number of his visitors from Girga had

---

89   The Arabic Life of Metropolitan Mena, 71–72.

increased significantly, and Metropolitan Mena desired to build a guest house for them. There was a plot of land nearby that he wished to buy, but the owner refused to sell.

Metropolitan Mena dedicated several liturgies specifically to this matter. After one such Liturgy, he handed his disciple a pitcher of holy water and instructed him to sprinkle the water over the entire plot. Not long afterward, the owner himself approached him with a desire to sell. Many donors came forward to donate, and the land was finally purchased.

One night, Metropolitan Mena was awakened by a hand pressing repeatedly upon his shoulder. He heard a familiar voice, "I want to stay here." When he opened his eyes, Metropolitan Mena saw Fr. Abdel Massih standing at his bedside.

The metropolitan threw the covers off, put on his glasses, and rose from his bed. Together, he and Fr. Abdel Massih left the room and walked to the newly acquired land.

Fr. Abdel Massih motioned with his cane, "Here is the nave of the church."

He walked further down the plot and began drawing on the ground with the stick he leaned on. "This," he continued, carving a large square into the soil, "is where you will build the altar."

He lifted the fringe of his tunic and ran back toward him. "Here is the door of the church," he said with an intent gaze, "and pay attention to the length and width of the building." He then conveyed to him the precise measurements he desired.

"And this," he declared with a single strike of his cane into the earth, "is the place where you will lay my body."

Metropolitan Mena stood in awe. The land was not going to be a guest house, after all. Fr. Abdel Massih wanted it to be a church, and he was drawing the plans himself!

"I want to be your neighbor," Fr. Abdel Massih smiled. "May the Lord be with you." He then vanished.

The metropolitan left the land and returned to his room with a single prayer in his heart, "Lord, send me the funds needed to complete the work of building a church for Your saint."

Only a few hours later, that very morning, he heard a knock at his door. His brother Aziz had arrived from their hometown of Rahmaniya Qibly. He handed him an envelope with 7,000 pounds. It happened that his family had sold some of their property in the city, and this was his share of the earnings. With a deep sigh of relief, he looked upward and whispered, "Thank You, my Lord. Thank You."[90]

The hand of the Lord moved with power and swiftness. The building rose exactly according to the instructions given by Fr. Abdel Massih himself. The altar was established, the icons were written, and two tombs were prepared; one was constructed to house the relics of Fr. Abdel Massih, and the other was reserved for Metropolitan Mena himself, should he repose while pursuing the life of solitude in Manahra.

---

90   The Arabic Life of Metropolitan Mena, 72–73.

The small church of Fr. Abdel Massih of the Monastery of St. Macarius in the village of Manahra, whose design was drawn by Fr. Abdel Massih himself, and conveyed by Fr. Abdel Massih personally to Metropolitan Mena

The Old Coffin

The appointed hour arrived to transfer the holy relics of Fr. Abdel Massih. After spending hours in prayer, Metropolitan Mena entered the new church in the stillness of the night and secured the door behind him. He proceeded slowly to the closed casket. Alone before the body, he got to his knees.

"Absolve me, my father," he whispered.

He extended his hands to the coffin, lifted the cover, and tenderly gathered the blessed bones of Fr. Abdel Massih. He arranged each one with great care inside the new casket.

After the relics were interred in the tomb, Metropolitan Mena left the original coffin in the church; he intended to decide its fate when morning came. All through the night, one question pressed upon his heart: What was to be done with the old coffin that had sheltered the holy relics of Fr. Abdel Massih for nearly two decades?

In the morning, his disciple, Awad Farag, made his way to the cell and was overjoyed to hear that the relics had been relocated.

"Come," Metropolitan Mena urged Awad, "let's see what we are going to do with his old coffin. Will we use it to stock candles? Or will we store the bottles of *abarka*[91] in it? What will we do with it?"

They entered the church and stood before the old coffin. But as they drew near, goosebumps completely overtook them; they heard the clear sound of a saw cutting through wood, finding its source from within the coffin itself.

They approached to listen, but quickly drew back. They witnessed the upper third of the coffin, together with its lid, separate into pieces and collapse of its own accord!

The sound of the sawing recurred once more. The lower portion of the coffin, including its base, was likewise severed into pieces.

When Fr. Kyrillos, the priest of the church, arrived and was told what had taken place, he asked to see for himself what had happened. Abdel Massih's old coffin had been reduced to nothing but a number of old wooden planks. He found that they were sawn clean into pieces and scattered across the floor. He was overcome with astonishment and began to spontaneously shout, "May the Lord's name be glorified!"

Metropolitan Mena told Awad, "The coffin disassembled on its own because Fr. Abdel Massih is the one who disassembled it. The Lord and Fr. Abdel Massih did not agree

---

91   Sacramental wine, used in the liturgical services of the Coptic Orthodox Church.

for anyone to extend their hand to it and repurpose it after it carried his body."

"What will you do with it?" Awad asked.

"We will collect the planks and bury them in the sand in my own tomb."[92]

Standing at the entrance to the church which Fr. Abdel Massih himself designed

---

92   The Arabic Life of Metropolitan Mena, 74–75.

Metropolitan Mena (center) stands next to his disciple Awad (far right) outside his cell during his period of solitude in Manahra

His Return to the Girga

His disciple Awad Farag Gayed explains:

His Holiness Pope Shenouda sent him a delegation of senior bishops in order to bring him back to Girga, because his spiritual children could not live without him. During this period, [His Holiness] often sent a papal vicar to Girga, but the people were not at rest. They would write a report to him and say, "Your Holiness, the people want Metropolitan Mena."

When [the delegation] went to him and spoke to him, you could hear the sound of his weeping from the road outside. He wept and sobbed uncontrollably.

They asked him, "What is the matter, Your Eminence?"

"I want to rest! I want to conclude my life in solitude! It's over—I'm now with Fr. Abdel Massih, my father and my beloved—it's over."

They said, "No, your children want you."

And so they took him, and he returned with great dignity.

Metropolitan Mena with the Papal Delegation

After a period of solitude spanning three years, seven months, and twenty-eight days, Metropolitan Mena was directed by Pope Shenouda III to return to Girga according to the requests of thousands. He celebrated the Feast of the Nativity in the Cathedral of Archangel Michael on the evening of Tuesday, January 6, 1981.

On Sunday, January 25, he stood at the lectern of the church of St. Mary in Girga with enthusiasm and explained the experiences he had witnessed during his time in solitude, from the moving of the relics, to the building of the church, to the miracles he heard from those he interviewed. He said:

> God willing, perhaps the Lord will allow me, and Fr. Abdel Massih of Manahra will look favorably on me; I will make a memorial for him here, and establish something through which we all may be blessed. Everything is in God's hands.
>
> If God wills, I will build, in the name of Fr. Abdel Massih, a shrine that will remain open at all times. I will move the altar of St. Pishoy to the church of the

Archangel [Michael] on the ground floor because it is more spacious, and I love Abba Pishoy. And when the small church is consecrated, it will bear the name of Fr. Abdel Massih of the Monastery of St. Macarius.

And perhaps God will allow me to bring a portion of his body here in Girga, so that Girga may be blessed through him. May God grant us benefit through his prayers.

From that night, Metropolitan Mena began contemplating the matter of bringing a portion of his relics.

He commissioned the iconostasis[93] for the small church and asked to add an icon of Fr. Abdel Massih. Under the icon, he designed a glass display cabinet, where Fr. Abdel Massih's relics could eventually be laid. He had a large octagonal wooden reliquary tube commissioned, lined with red velvet.

The Relics of Fr. Abdel Massih
Come to Girga Miraculously

The Great Fast in 1981 commenced, and Metropolitan Mena travelled to Manahra,[94] taking with him the new reliquary. He prayed constantly for God to allow Fr. Abdel Massih to appear to him, or to show him a sign, to give him permission to remove for himself a portion of the relics.

---

93   The iconostasis, derived from the Greek words εἰκών (icon) and στάσις (standing), is a wall or partition adorned with icons that separates the nave from the sanctuary in the Orthodox Church. It serves both a liturgical and symbolic function, representing the boundary between the heavenly and the earthly realms, and typically features consecrated icons of the Lord Christ, the Mother of God, the apostles, angels, martyrs, and saints, arranged in a hierarchical order.

94   With Manahra close to his heart, Metropolitan Mena usually spent the entire Great Fast there.

He fasted. He prayed. He secluded himself completely. And yet, Fr. Abdel Massih did not appear, and the fast was coming to a close.

He whispered dejectedly, "Fr. Abdel Massih, I'm not used to you not answering me when I call you. What's going on? Are you upset with me?"

Matters in Girga required him, and he began receiving multiple messages pressuring him to return. Metropolitan Mena began to weep. He desperately asked the saint to come to him. But he did not.

Finally, on the last night before his return to Girga, his entire room became as bright as day; inexplicable light filled the cell. And out of a cloud of fragrant incense, Fr. Abdel Massih emerged.

Metropolitan Mena rejoiced. "What's the matter, Fr. Abdel Massih? Are you mad at me?"

The saint shook his head and smiled. The spiritual father and son spoke for a while.

"You can go ahead and return to Girga," Fr. Abdel Massih began, "but leave the tube here."

The metropolitan obeyed the command. He entered the church, carrying the empty tube in his arms. He left it beside the saint's body. He then returned to Girga and led the services of Holy Week, the Feast of the Resurrection, and the Feast of the Ascension.

It was the Saturday following the Feast of the Ascension, June 6, 1981. The dark room was once again engulfed in light. Fr. Abdel Massih had come.

"I brought you the gift you wanted," he told him. "It is in the tube. I also laid it in the place you designated as a shrine for me. Thank you." And he immediately vanished.

Metropolitan Mena hastily slipped on his shoes and rushed out of his cell. He all but flew down the stairs. When he entered the church, he found himself immobilized. The tube he left behind in Manahra was now here, before him, inside the glass display cabinet.

He combed through his keys; he searched for the single key, which only he possessed, that could open the cabinet. When he found it, his hands shook as he fitted it into the lock. At last, the hinged door opened, and he scooped the reliquary tube into his arms.

He knew he needed to open the wooden tube, which was sealed shut with screws. He brought a screwdriver and undid each one, though his hands were barely steady enough to turn them. When, at last, the cover was lifted, he gazed down in astonishment. At the bottom of the tube lay a fragment from the body of Fr. Abdel Massih.

He sat in silence, bewildered, for several minutes. Finally, he uttered, "Fr. Abdel Massih, did you, yourself, bring back the tube with your holy relics inside? You carried it yourself from Manahra all the way to Girga? How could that be?"

Metropolitan Mena returned the reliquary to its display case and instantly found for himself the flask of the Holy Myron.[95] He pulled aside the veil of the sanctuary. In intense joy, he cried out, pouring and smearing the Holy Myron on

---

95   The Holy Myron (Greek: Μύρων, meaning "myrrh" or "perfume") is the oil of the highest sanctity in the Christian Church. This sacred oil contains the very spices placed on the body of the Lord Jesus Christ during His burial. These spices, meticulously preserved and blended with pure olive oil by the apostles, were distributed among them for use in their evangelistic endeavors. It is the holy anointing oil utilized in the Mysteries of Baptism and Chrismation, for the indwelling of the Holy Spirit. It is also used for sanctification and consecration of altars, icons and altar vessels.

the altar, "I consecrate this altar with this Holy Myron for the name of St. Abdel Massih of the Monastery of St. Macarius…"

The next morning, Sunday, June 7, 1981, he celebrated the Divine Liturgy on that same altar amidst the utmost joy of Girga's people, who gladly welcomed Fr. Abdel Massih among them.

His Eminence would forever regard the day on which the reliquary arrived—brought personally by Fr. Abdel Massih, containing a portion of his holy relics—as a great feast for the church in Girga. He commemorated the miracle annually on the Sunday between the Feast of the Ascension and the Feast of Pentecost.

Each year, on that day, the church receives thousands of visitors from every part of the diocese, as well as from neighboring and distant towns. There are countless miracles that are reported to have occurred on that particular day.

Metropolitan Mena describes:

Never did I imagine that Fr. Abdel Massih, himself, would bless us by carrying the reliquary containing his own relics and offering a blessing with his own hands to the people of Girga. I thank You, O Lord, first of all, for You have granted me what I longed for and even more. And I thank Fr. Abdel Massih for his great act and for the blessing he personally bestowed upon the people of Girga.

Metropolitan Mena firmly instructed that the details concerning the miraculous transfer of the relics of Fr. Abdel Massih be kept undisclosed until the time of his own repose.[96]

---

96   The Arabic Life of Metropolitan Mena, 89–91.

The relics of Fr. Abdel Massih of the Monastery of St. Macarius, which Fr. Abdel Massih himself brought from the village of Manahra to the church of St. Mary in Girga. Displayed also, to the left of the relics, are a tunic and a walking stick which belonged to him.

Discipleship Never Ends

Though a portion of the relics was now in Girga, he showed his faithfulness to his spiritual father by visiting Manahra every so often for retreat. He would sit on the ground under the body of Fr. Abdel Massih, especially if problems arose in the diocese. He would raise his eyes to God, asking for the prayers of Fr. Abdel Massih, who would appear to him immediately.

Hegumen Hedra Aziz from Girga relates:

One time, His Eminence was on a trip to Cairo. When he was returning back to Girga, he fell ill. He was admitted to the Archangel Hospital in Assiut. When Abba Mikhail of Assiut heard of his coming, he immediately arose and went to check on him.

At the hospital, Abba Mikhail heard Abba Mena speaking about Fr. Abdel Massih. He asked him about the last time he saw Fr. Abdel Massih.

His Eminence Metropolitan Mena replied, "Yesterday!"

When he noticed that the people turned to him and exchanged surprised glances, he changed the subject and asked to be taken to the car.[97]

For discipleship never ends, though there is separation in the flesh.

At times, Fr. Abdel Massih himself solved the matter, even if it seemed impossible to solve.

One day, a man from Samalut came to Metropolitan Mena asking for a letter of recommendation so that he

---

97   The Arabic Life of Metropolitan Mena, 131

could apply for a job at a blanket factory owned by one of the metropolitan's spiritual sons. Metropolitan Mena wrote the letter right away. Although he did not know the man personally, he always took joy in helping others whenever he could.

Two days later, Metropolitan Mena received a phone call from the factory owner. The man had altered the letter, turning it into a letter of guarantee, and falsely claimed that Metropolitan Mena had approved him to take goods worth 60,000 pounds. The factory owner explained that he refused to release anything until he could confirm the matter directly with the metropolitan.

Metropolitan Mena ended the phone call, visibly upset, and went into his cell to pray.

Those who listened in on the call found that, no more than ten minutes later, they heard a loud noise outside. They rushed out and were stunned to find the same man who had altered the letter thrown into the courtyard of the church of Fr. Abdel Massih, as though he had been hurled there.

They brought the man to Metropolitan Mena. Trembling, he ran toward him, begging for forgiveness.

Metropolitan Mena calmly said to him, "I never harmed you. Why did you want to harm me?" He then forgave the man and sent him away.

Those who witnessed the incident asked in amazement, "Why did this man come here? Who brought him? And why was he thrown in front of the church of Fr. Abdel Massih?"

Metropolitan Mena explained, "When I entered my cell, I said to Fr. Abdel Massih, 'Where am I supposed to get sixty thousand pounds? You deal with this.'" He said that Fr. Abdel Massih immediately went to the man's house, seized him by his shirt, and threw him into the church courtyard.

The amount of love these two elders had for one another was truly incomprehensible. The distance between heaven and earth never encumbered their relationship.

CHAPTER SEVEN

His Spiritual Canon and Ascesis

His Prayers

Metropolitan Mena was girded in the Holy Schema[98] since his tonsure in 1939. The wearing of the Holy Schema carries with it its own rigorous monastic canon:

✤ Praying all 151 Psalms each day.

✤ Reciting the Praises of the Prophets (comprising twenty-five sections).

✤ Chanting the Midnight Praises, including the Doxologies, Tadakias, and the Four Canticles.

✤ Reading the entirety of the Holy Bible within a prescribed cycle, typically every 40 to 50 days, according to the discipline set by his spiritual father.

✤ Adhering to a vow of silence to the greatest extent possible.

---

98   The Holy Schema (derived from the Greek word, σχῆμα, "schema," meaning shape or form) is a distinctive belt-like object made of intricately plaited strips of leather that wrap around the chest and back. It features two prominent leather crosses, one positioned on the chest and the other on the small of the back, along with twelve smaller crosses spaced evenly along the chest, shoulders, back, and abdomen. This leather girdle has roots all the way back to St. Anthony the Great, who was given the Schema by an angel. The monastic girded in the Holy Schema is an ascetic who has attained the highest degrees of spirituality.

✤   Fulfilling a fixed canon of prostrations (*metanoias*).

At the beginning of his monastic life, his canon comprised 2,000 prostrations a day. Metropolitan Mena upheld this throughout his years in Manahra and continued to cling to it even after his return to Girga. In the 1990s, when illness and physical weakness took hold of him, his canon was reduced to 500 prostrations a day.

Metropolitan Mena viewed each prostration he completed as an expression of contrition, submission, penitence, and the longing to obtain sanctification and absolution from the Lord. The prostration was a falling with Christ under the weight of the cross. When his forehead touches the ground, he remembers that he was created from dust and will return to it.

He would begin his day at 1:00 a.m. Once he awoke, he began praying the Midnight Hour of the Agpeya, which he lovingly called "the meeting of the Bridegroom."

Throughout the night, he would pray, stretching his hands toward heaven. He remembered every person, by name, who had asked him to pray for them. He would intercede for the Church and her clergy. He would remember the sick and the souls of the departed. He would pray for the peace and tranquility of the world and the people therein, asking the Lord to resolve problems, to lift inflation, famine, and plague. He would remember the poor, the needy, the unemployed, the students, the monastics, the crops, the grass, the waters of the Nile, and those entrusted with the affairs of the country.

His prayers lasted until 6:00 in the morning, though they frequently continued well past that time.

Metropolitan Mena standing in his cell, girded in the Holy Schema. He wore it constantly under his cassock.

His Fasting

His spiritual canon was to abstain from food and drink until sunset daily. As a newly-tonsured monk, he found himself beginning to suffer from low blood pressure and extreme weight loss due to excessive fasting. One of the elders of the monastery, an Ethiopian monk, instructed him, "Add one hour of fasting every three months." He followed this until he could abstain till sunset without feeling any weakness.

As for his spiritual rule in the Great Fast, he abstained from food and water for two days at a time. The amount of food he would eat on the third day would be described as insufficient for a toddler. He would then abstain again for two more days.

Fr. Yacoub Attia, priest of the church of the Holy Virgin Mary in Girga, reminisces:

We sat with His Eminence at the table, and he would pretend to eat with us. We would see him merely put his finger into his plate of cooked vegetables and bread, from the outside.

His Eminence would be content with just a few spoonfuls of salad. Though he saw us eating, in order to escape and leave the table, he would say, "You are not eating, you are embarrassed because of me," And he would rise from the table right away.

Because of this, he became skin and bones; he was one of the Spirit-borne anchorites. Since 1977, when he began his solitude, he did not taste meat at all; even when he left, he considered himself bound to the same canon of solitude. During the days of his final illness and weakness, he refused to eat meat despite the doctors' advice. Under pressure, he allowed himself only one meal of fish a day on the days when eating fish was permitted.[99]

He was keen on guarding and protecting the new priests he ordained. When they came to spend the first forty days with him at the episcopal residence after their ordination, he would not allow them to attend the grand ordination celebrations that people held for them. He would say to the people, "Leave them alone, so that you do not waste these holy days for them in vain things."

And yet, at the same time, he was incredibly benevolent, saying to the priests staying with him, "The refrigerator is full. There is no restriction! Whoever wants to eat something may take it."

He drank tea only once a day so that the habit would not gain control over him. He would add a little water to it to remove its taste, its aroma, and its flavor.

---

99   The Arabic Life of Metropolitan Mena, 146.

CHAPTER EIGHT

His Spiritual Gifts and Miracles

Metropolitan Mena lived in constant struggle and spiritual preparation. He entered into the knowledge of God, and God, in turn, led him into the depths of the spiritual life. He came to be counted among the Spirit-borne anchorites, and for a period, he was regarded as the chief among them.

By keeping his eyes on the Lord, he forgot himself and grew in the spirit, subjecting his body to his soul. The heaviness of his material body gradually gave way, and the spirit prevailed over the flesh. The body itself became lightened, purified, and refined. As a result, he rose above the ordinary limits of nature and the constraints of earthly gravity, and so he possessed an enlightened heart and a discerning eye, which was capable of perceiving what was hidden from others.

As with the other anchorites, his guardian angel would accompany and bear him wherever God willed, without hindrance or obstacle.

His period of solitude was a time marked by his active participation in services and gatherings with the Spirit-borne anchorites. After he began pursuing the solitary life in 1977, he was told of the desire of the anchorites to celebrate the Divine Liturgy in the church of St. Mary in Manahra. He celebrated the Liturgy for them, per their request.[100]

Then, in 1978, Metropolitan Mena prayed another Liturgy for the anchorites. He expounds further:

> I know someone honest and truthful, who prefers that his name not be mentioned, who admits to having prayed the Divine Liturgy with the saintly anchorites. He himself was the leading presbyter, and he communed them of the Holy Mysteries, for an ordained priest was not numbered among them; the anchorite priest who was with them had recently departed to Paradise. For this reason, they took this person with them so that he might raise the Gifts for them and give them Communion. He relayed that he did not know how he was taken with them to the heart of the desert. He also said that after the distribution [of the Holy Eucharist], he was transported back to his village the same way he left it. They left him with promises and commands which he refuses to reveal.[101]

Based on conversations between Metropolitan Mena and his disciples, where there was an occasional slip of the tongue, it was revealed that it was he himself who was taken by the anchorites into the depths of the desert in 1978. He had spoken in the same manner as St. Paul the Apostle, who describes, "I know a man in Christ who fourteen years ago—whether in the body I do not know, or whether out of the body I do not know, God knows—such a one was caught up to the third heaven."[102]

---

100 *Al-Anba Mena al-Sa'eh wa-l-Aba' al-Sowah* [Abba Mena the Anchorite and the Anchorite Fathers] by Children of Abba Mena, published under the auspices of the Diocese of Girga, Bahjurah, and Farshut, 13–14.

101 The Arabic Life of Fr. Abdel Massih, 36.

102 2 Cor 12:2.

As for the "promises and commands," he was told that he would be numbered with the anchorites.

Metropolitan Mena had prayed the Divine Liturgy more than five times with the Spirit-borne anchorites, and he himself presided over prayers. He explains that there is a mountain between the Monastery of St. Anthony and the Monastery of St. Paul in the Eastern Wilderness, which is inhabited by these anchorites, and that he would pray with them there.

The anchorites, he explains, took him to this mountain, where, within it, he found a chapel hewn out of the rock. There he beheld the anchorites waiting for him inside the chapel. Some covered and concealed their bodies with a few pieces of coarse fabric, others had extremely lengthy beards that the Lord willed to grow to such lengths to serve as their covering. Among them, he even found a childhood friend of his. After the Divine Liturgy, they returned him to his place.[103]

---

103 This instance of His Eminence's personal experience is included a video interview labelled, "A Talk of Memories," produced by the Monastery of Archangel Michael in East Girga.

Travelling to America with His Anchoritic Gifts

He never boarded a plane in the span of his lifetime, and yet he was able, through the gifts of God, to be physically present anywhere in the world to better minister to his flock.

Fr. Pola al-Gawargi, the disciple of Metropolitan Mena, recounts how he knows a family from Girga who immigrated to California. Their son, Mena, who was four years old at the time, suddenly lost his eyesight. He was taken from hospital to hospital, and from physician to physician. They telephoned their acquaintances in Girga, asking them to lift prayers for Mena's eyesight to be restored. The family sent a message to His Eminence stating the following: "We ask that you pray for our son Mena, and that you may send him Fr. Abdel Massih to heal him."

Reading the message, he looked up through his glasses, "And why can't I go to him?" Those around him assumed he was joking.

Back in the United States, in the middle of the night, Mena's parents took shifts in the hospital looking after him. The child was instructed not to move, and his parents kept watch, ensuring the doctor's orders were followed.

Mena's parents unexpectedly saw Metropolitan Mena opening the door and walking into the hospital room, dressed in his white liturgical vestments. He reassured them.

Then, he walked over to the hospital bed and tapped Mena's eyes with the cross in his hand. He whispered a few short prayers and anointed his eyes with a bottle of oil he produced from his pocket. He then vanished into thin air before their eyes. Mena was healed.[104]

---

104 *Al-Anba Mena al-Sa'eh wa-l-Aba' al-Sowah* [Abba Mena the Anchorite and the Anchorite Fathers], 18.

Travelling to Kuwait with His Anchoritic Gifts

Mrs. J.A., a Muslim woman from Girga, who was very familiar with the greatness of Metropolitan Mena's spiritual stature, used to say about him that he was "one of God's great servants, whose supplications God answers." She and her husband and children would consult Metropolitan Mena about every matter of their lives, and continually ask for his blessing and prayers.

When her husband was offered a work contract in Kuwait, they went to His Eminence to ask his opinion about traveling. He agreed, blessed their decision, and prayed for them.

The family went to Kuwait and settled in an apartment. This apartment, as they would later discover, was inhabited by a demonic, unclean spirit, which they referred to as a *tabiᶜa* [a pursuing spirit]. It turned their life into utter torment. The wife sent a message to her family in Girga, begging for help, and asked them to go to His Eminence at the episcopal residence; it was he who had agreed for them to move to Kuwait, anyway. She asked her family to have him remove this evil spirit.

That evening, this woman and her family saw Metropolitan Mena enter their apartment in Kuwait.

She would later say, "I do not know how he came."

He then seized the demon, bound it, wrapped it in a blanket, and sprinkled the apartment with holy water. He then carried the blanket, with the demon bound within, and threw it into a drainage canal that was in front of the building. He then vanished.

She informed her family of what had happened, and they went to the metropolitan to offer abundant thanks.

Years later, this woman came to the Monastery of the Archangel, along with her husband, her children, and her whole family. They were rejoicing, with ululations filling every courtyard of the monastery. They presented Metropolitan Mena with a valuable gift and offered their thanksgiving, because he had delivered them from "the jinn" that had turned their life into misery. Following this, they lived in peace and stability.[105]

He Materialized Right in Front of Me!

Mr. Osama Mishil Adly al-Khabbaz records:

It was summer vacation. I was in college and had successfully completed my second year. I was serving in the summer camp at the church of the Holy Virgin Mary in Girga. One day, after the camp ended around 9:30 p.m., I went for a walk on Mohamed Farid Street in al-Hawza with one of the [church] servants.

Because my eyesight is weak, and because there was a house whose foundations were being dug, I did not see the pit, and I fell into it. I found myself overwhelmed with great distress, and I felt deeply troubled at the state [of my eyesight]. I climbed out with the help of the servant, and then I took my distance from him to weep in private; my soul was very heavy within me.

I found myself heading to the episcopal residence; His Eminence was my source of comfort and consolation. I went, even though I knew that he would be in his cell completing his prayers.

When I reached the residence, I entered the inner hall. The lights were left turned on, and all the interior doors

---

105 The Arabic Life of Metropolitan Mena, 161–162.

within the hall were closed.

While I was standing there in deep sorrow, I suddenly found His Eminence in front of me. He did not enter through a door, but materialized in the room, right in front of me!

I burst into tears and told him what had occurred. He embraced me. I sobbed, "Did Your Eminence see what happened to me?"

He prayed for me, and I found that the distress, sadness, and exhaustion abandoned me.

I said to him, "I love you, Your Eminence."

He replied tenderly, "I know, my son."

Then I was astonished to see His Eminence disappear from before me. How? I do not know; he vanished just as suddenly as he had appeared! I was overcome with fear. I immediately left the residence, closed the door behind me, and was still in a state of shock.

The very next day, knowing that His Eminence usually descends from his cell at around 4:30 in the afternoon, I went to him and found him sitting at his desk.

I greeted him, "Your Eminence, I wanted to thank you for what you did for me last night. Your prayers saved me. I was sad, and exhausted, and crying."

He instantly replied, "I did not see you last night."

I answered, "I came here last night, Your Eminence! And I met Your Eminence, but I'm not entirely sure how you appeared before me."

His Eminence responded, "I do not know anything about this, nor about what happened to you."

I became afraid. I entreated him, "Forgive me! Forgive me, Your Eminence!"

I was filled with confusion. I excused myself to leave, giving my back to the door as I walked out, out of respect for him.

He then looked up at me and said, "My son, if someone comes to the residence at that hour, before he leaves, he must turn off the lights!"

At that moment, I understood immediately that it was indeed His Eminence whom I met the previous night.

I could not control myself; I quickly fell at his feet, began kissing them, and cried out, "Forgive me, Your Eminence. You were the one who met me last night! You prayed for me and took away my worry and my exhaustion! I do not know where you came from or how you disappeared. I was so confused!"

His Eminence Metropolitan Mena then strictly ordered me not to speak about this, and I promised him that I would only mention this story until the time was appropriate, that is, after his departure.

I came to know that Metropolitan Mena was one of the great Spirit-borne anchorites. And the time has come to speak. May Your name, O Lord, be glorified in Your saints.[106]

I Did Not Find Him

Mr. Wahba Girgis Megalaa, who was a disciple and servant of His Eminence Metropolitan Mena for more than thirty years, says:

When His Eminence's health began to decline, I began to sleep and spend the night at the episcopal residence, in the room next to His Eminence's cell. The doctors instructed him

---

106 *Al-Anba Mena al-Sa'eh wa-l-Aba' al-Sowah* [Abba Mena the Anchorite and the Anchorite Fathers] by Children of Abba Mena, published under the auspices of the Diocese of Girga, Bahjurah, and Farshut, 38–39.

to drink a cup of milk with his medication. I woke up early and asked His Eminence's permission to prepare the cup of milk, and he asked me to postpone it.

After a while, I knocked on the door of the cell to seek his permission to prepare the milk, but I did not find him in the cell.

I went to the bathroom. He was not there. I searched for him in all the rooms of the residence. I did not find him on the middle floor, nor on the ground floor, nor even on the roof. I did not find him! I went to the church courtyard, where the churches were still closed, and I did not find him.

In my bewilderment, I went back to his cell once more.

And I found him! Yes, I found him after more than twenty minutes.

I said to His Eminence, "Where were you, Your Eminence?"

He replied, "Your questions annoy me. Go bring me that cup of milk."

And I realized then that he was one of the anchorites.

Do Not Knock on the Door!

Mr. Wahba Girgis Megalaa continues recounting his memories:

Also, one night, I was in the room adjacent to His Eminence's cell, spending the night there. In the middle of the night, I awoke to the sound of chanting and praising, and the sound of a bell tolling. The light in His Eminence's cell was turned off.

I initially thought that the church had begun the prayers of the Divine Liturgy. I looked from the balcony; there were no churches open at this hour; it was shortly after midnight!

Upon inspection, I realized that the sounds and voices were coming from His Eminence's cell. I listened on in astonishment. After some time, I knocked on the door of the cell and said to him, "Your Eminence, are you speaking with someone?"

His Eminence replied from within, "Stop this talk! Do not let me hear this from you again. Go prepare breakfast for the fathers who are here!"

I replied, "Who are they, Your Eminence?"

His Eminence retorted, "Enough! Go now, and do not knock on the door again."[107]

Tidying the Cell

Mr. Ibrahim Ayoub Meshreki, one of Metropolitan Mena's close spiritual sons, recounts how on one occasion he stayed with Metropolitan Mena for three days. During that time, he remembered supporting the metropolitan as they walked together toward the outer room of his cell.

Suddenly, the metropolitan stopped, looked upward, and smiled faintly, "Why have you all increased in number so much?"

When those with him asked about the identity of those he was addressing, he answered simply, "The anchorites."

Throughout his stay, Mr. Ibrahim and those with him took it upon themselves to tidy the metropolitan's cell. He noticed an extraordinary amount of hair on the ground, hair of various lengths, colors, and textures. When pressed, Metropolitan Mena explained that many of the anchorites frequented his cell and that the hair had fallen from them.

---

107 Ibid., 40–41.

At his admission of the truth, the hair started to disappear before their eyes. They quickly scrambled to save only a few strands, which they preserved as a blessing.[108]

Another Story

Hegumen Fr. Abraam Youssef, priest of the church of St. George in Raqaqna, relates:

My relationship with our saintly father, Metropolitan Mena, was close. I spent my forty-day retreat after my ordination at the episcopal residence with him.

I asked His Eminence, "Your Eminence, are there currently any anchorites?"

He answered with confidence, "Yes."

I inquired, "And how many anchorite fathers are there, Your Eminence?"

He replied, "Their number is eighteen or nineteen anchorites."

And when he began to realize what he had said, he started waving his hands, refusing to continue, as though he was unaware of what had slipped from him while speaking.[109]

---

108 Ibid., 17.

109 Ibid., 17.

Prophesying the Tonsure of His Disciple

When Metropolitan Mena's longtime spiritual child during his days in Manahra, Girgis Gaber Ibrahim, sought his blessing to enter the monastic life, the metropolitan told him plainly, "They will name you Pola. You will become a monk, and then I will take you."

Indeed, after Girgis joined the Monastery of St. George in Khatatba and completed his novitiate, the late Bishop Bemwa, the abbot of the monastery, gathered the novices who were to be tonsured and asked each of them to choose the name he desired.

When he reached Brother Girgis, he asked him, "What would you like them to name you?"

Brother Girgis replied, "Whatever Your Grace sees fit."

Bishop Bemwa answered, "We will name you Pola."

Thus, he was tonsured with the name Pola, exactly as Metropolitan Mena had prophesied.

Six years later, Metropolitan Mena visited Pope Shenouda III and requested a monk who could assist him in the ministry and become his disciple. Fr. Pola was chosen, and the metropolitan's prophecy was fulfilled to the fullest extent.[110]

He's a Saintly Man!

One day, Metropolitan Mena looked at the framed photo of Bishop Macarius of Qena, which hung on the wall of the episcopal reception hall.

"He's a saintly man," he announced. "And he loves prayer so much! He will depart while praying the Liturgy."

---

110 The Arabic Life of Metropolitan Mena, 141.

The very next day, on Sunday, February 3, 1991, the news came by telephone from the Diocese of Qena: "Bishop Macarius departed this morning while standing at the altar during the Divine Liturgy."[111]

Protect us!

Fr. Pola al-Gawargi remembers it being a cool September night. He fell asleep but was awakened at 2:00 a.m., panicked; he heard Metropolitan Mena screaming from his room. He ran to him, thinking he had hurt himself.

The closer he got to his room, the clearer he could hear the agony in his voice. "Take it away from us, Lord," he kept repeating, "No, Lord! Take it away!"

He listened closely, with his ear to the door, "Take it away, Lord! What a loss! What a great loss!"

He was being communicated something. Something disastrous was about to happen.

Later that day, he received news that two airplanes had been hijacked and had crashed into the World Trade Center in New York.[112]

I Already Know

Mr. Malak Anwar Abdel Malak, who served Metropolitan Mena in his final days, remembers:

On one occasion, he informed us that he wished to celebrate the Divine Liturgy. We asked him, "Where would you like to pray, Your Eminence?"

---

111   Ibid., 141.

112   Ibid., 140.

He replied, "We will pray at the Monastery of St. Mena in Mariout."

We traveled to the monastery and celebrated the Liturgy there. After its conclusion, one of the monks approached His Eminence and said, "Your Eminence, His Grace Bishop Gregorios is visiting the monastery. Would Your Eminence like to see him?"

His Eminence looked at us and smiled a beautiful smile and said, "That is why I came!"

At the time, we did not understand his words. We entered the reception room and waited for Bishop Gregorios to join us. Soon after, Bishop Gregorios entered with his servant. Metropolitan Mena rose to his feet, and the two greeted and embraced one another warmly. We brought a chair for Metropolitan Mena and placed it directly facing Bishop Gregorios, and the two sat opposite each other.

A profound silence followed. It lasted nearly twenty or thirty minutes. No words were exchanged. Metropolitan Mena and Bishop Gregorios simply gazed at one another, occasionally nodding at each other. We remained seated, and we were perplexed by what we were witnessing.

At the end of this time, we noticed Metropolitan Mena's eyes fill with tears, and he began to weep. Fr. Pola and I hurried to him and asked, "Your Eminence, is something troubling you? What is the matter? Is there a problem?"

"No, no," he replied. "There is nothing wrong."

Then we saw Metropolitan Mena remove his turban, bow his head before Bishop Gregorios, and say, "Bless me."

We later returned to the Monastery of the Archangel. This encounter took place toward the end of September 2001. On October 24, 2001, we received the news that

Bishop Gregorios had departed to Paradise.

Knowing the depth of Metropolitan Mena's love for him, we struggled with how to tell him. We tried to approach the subject gently, without revealing everything at once.

Finally, he looked at me and asked, "Malak, what is the matter?"

Fr. Pola and I exchanged glances, then said, "His Grace Bishop Gregorios has gone to heaven today."

He looked at us calmly and said, "May the Lord support us through his prayers. I already know."

Only later did we understand the reason for his earlier tears: he knew that Bishop Gregorios was nearing his departure.[113]

---

113 Video Interview taken from *Al-Zāhid: Suṭūr min Ḥayāt Muthallath Al-Raḥamāt Al-Anbā Mīnā Muṭrān Jirjā* [The Ascetic: Lines from the Life of the Thrice-Blessed Abba Mena, Metropolitan of Girga], on November 6, 2025.

*Photograph from the meeting between Bishop Gregorios
and Metropolitan Mena*

Praying in the Monastery of Muharraq

Fr. Isidore of Muharraq adds to the instances of Metropolitan Mena's gifts of clairvoyance, remembering how, in September of 2003, before the metropolitan's repose by about two months, he visited him in the Monastery of Archangel Michael with his biological brother, Fr. Elisha of Muharraq.

Fr. Isidore told Metropolitan Mena, "In June, the monks and I noticed that the chapel named after St. George in our monastery was used to celebrate a Liturgy; the altar was covered in water. The vessels were left wet after washing, and possessed the smell of fragrance. The clouds of incense were still in the air. We think the anchorites prayed there."

He squinted at Fr. Isidore and nodded, "Yes, they are the anchorite fathers, and I prayed with them at your monastery, the Monastery of Muharraq, on that very day."

He proceeded to relate the exact date the Liturgy was prayed, though Fr. Isidore did not mention it to him.

Upon realizing his slip of the tongue, he attempted to change the subject immediately. He hurriedly glanced at Fr. Elisha's chest and clutched the leather cross that hung around his neck.

He snickered to Fr. Elisha, "This belongs to your brother."

The cross around Fr. Elisha's neck was indeed Fr. Isidore's. He lent it to him, back at the monastery, before making the drive to Girga![114]

---

114 *Al-Anba Mena al-Sa'eh wa-l-Aba' al-Sowah* [Abba Mena the Anchorite and the Anchorite Fathers] by Children of Abba Mena, published under the auspices of the Diocese of Girga, Bahjurah, and Farshut, 27–28.

Did He Come to You?

About a month before his repose, while several monks sat in his presence, it was noticed that His Eminence slowly leaned on the table before him, placed his head between his hands, and became completely motionless. It was understood that he grew tired and needed a moment's rest.

A photograph of Metropolitan Mena, taken at the Monastery of Archangel Michael in East Girga, in which the flesh seems to be at rest. However, at the same time this photograph was taken, his physical presence was confirmed to be in another place, irrespective of distance.

He sat in that position for more than half an hour. Abruptly, he lifted his head with all energy and vitality, smiling and chuckling like a child.

Only seconds passed before the telephone rang, and a person known to everyone in the gathering, living in Hurghada (about 125 miles away), called to specifically inquire, "Did His Eminence come to you? He was just with me a few seconds ago; we just spent over half an hour talking together! Did he come to you?"[115]

Sounds After Midnight

Mr. A.A., who serves in the church of Archangel Michael in Girga, explains that he is the baker of the Qorban for the church. One night, while waiting for the dough to rise in the kitchen adjacent to the episcopal residence, he walked outside

---

115 The Arabic Life of Metropolitan Mena, 160.

and passed by the part of the building where Metropolitan Mena's cell was located. It was well after midnight.

As he walked down the sidewalk, he heard the most angelic, melodic hymns coming from the metropolitan's room; he had never heard such beautiful prayers in his life. Looking up toward the cell, over the balcony, he noticed an intense, supernatural light bursting through the blinds of the window.

He froze. He stood and listened. He could not comprehend how praises, which he initially assumed were coming from a cassette player, could possibly sound so beautiful. But the more he listened, the clearer the sounds became, and he began to understand that there was indeed a group of people inside the cell, praising alongside Metropolitan Mena.

But no visitors were permitted at that hour.

A few minutes later, the window of the balcony flew open. The heavenly light vanished, and the sounds of praise fell silent. Metropolitan Mena extended his head out of the window and glared, "Leave. Now."

He ordered that the baker not speak of his encounters with these "visitors" until after his repose.[116]

On the Appearance of Anchorites in the Form of Doves

Those close to Metropolitan Mena often told of his ability to appear and move in ways that defied ordinary explanation. Among these was his appearance and travel in the form of a dove of light. This manner was long associated in the tradition of the Church with the saints and Spirit-borne anchorites.

---

116 Ibid., 163.

The late Bishop Gregorios spoke about this openly in an audio-recorded sermon delivered on the eve of Sunday, March 20, 1988, at the church of Archangel Michael in Girga, saying:

> Angels often appear in the form of stars, while the righteous saints appear in the form of doves. Even during the days of the apparition of the Holy Virgin in Zeitoun, we saw doves, and we saw stars. The stars are angels, radiant above the roof of the church, while the doves are the spirits of the saints.

Pope Shenouda III adds in the weekly sermon he delivered on the occasion of the apparition of the Holy Virgin Saint Mary over her church in the district of Warraq on Wednesday, December 23, 2009:

> It is possible for the Holy Virgin to appear... but what, then, of the flock of doves that was seen soaring in the sky [with her]? They are the souls of the righteous holy ones, or the spirits of the saints, who follow the Virgin and greet her at her apparition.

What was This Dove?

Mr. Ayman Helmy Zaki, a timber merchant from Sheikh al-Arab in Girga had two daughters, and he had a deep desire and hope that the Lord would grant him a son. He went with his wife to Metropolitan Mena at the Monastery of the Archangel and asked him to pray for them, that God might grant them a son.

He prayed for them and said, "God willing, the Lord will give you a son." His wife miraculously gave birth to a son in the month of July, whom they named Andrew.

Because of the summer heat, the family would take their newborn and sleep in the room facing the street, as it had better air circulation. As they readied themselves to sleep, they noticed, on several nights, a dove of white light, with a size many folds that of a regular bird, landing across the street, directly before the window to Andrew's room. The dove would come at 11:30 p.m. and would stand in front of the house for over half an hour, at the same time daily, for forty consecutive days.

Ayman grew more perplexed with each passing day. What was this dove? Why was it coming at the same time every single night? When he told his friends about it, they said that it might be an apparition of one of the saints or martyrs, or of the Holy Virgin Mary.

Though he had grown accustomed to the appearance of this dove, Ayman knew he needed to get a closer look at this mysterious dove. The opportunity indeed came at the conclusion of the forty days.

The dove came on schedule, at 11:30 p.m., but strangely, it began to circle the house. It was much bigger than the times Ayman had seen it previously. It was shining with light.

When it landed in front of him, Ayman saw that this dove possessed the face of Metropolitan Mena, but the body of a dove. He saw the metropolitan's piercing eyes, his thick glasses, his white beard. He even wore his white monastic cowl, covered in crosses. But he had the body of a dove!

His daughter Marina was standing beside him on the balcony, and she cried out loudly, "Abba Mena, Daddy! Abba Mena, Daddy!"

Ayman stood in sheer astonishment, covered in goosebumps. He felt like he had suddenly become mute, and he was unable to open his mouth and yell for his wife to see what he was seeing.

For a whole five minutes, he stood before them. They understood that Metropolitan Mena's appearance to them, showing them his face in such a marvelous sight, was to purge them from the confusion and mystery that gripped them over the last forty days. Ayman later visited Metropolitan Mena and told him what he saw. He confirmed to Ayman that what he saw was true, but strictly adjured him never to speak of what he saw publicly until he reposed.[117]

Where is His Eminence?

In June of 2001, Metropolitan Mena was carried to the Monastery of Archangel Michael in East Girga, as he wished to spend his remaining days in silence and solitude. His health began to deteriorate, and he lost the ability to walk on his own. Though illness began to manifest, and the flesh began to weaken, the spirit was very much youthful and light.

On more than one occasion, the monks of the monastery would search for him, and yet they would be unable to find him, despite his inability to walk. They would search for him anxiously, and after some time, they would often find him in a place far from where he originally was.

Fr. Pola al-Gawargi recounts that one day there was a malfunction in the air-conditioning unit of Metropolitan Mena's cell. As a result, a room in the retreat house was

---

117 *Al-Anba Mena al-Sa'eh wa-l-Aba' al-Sowah* [Abba Mena the Anchorite and the Anchorite Fathers] by Children of Abba Mena, published under the auspices of the Diocese of Girga, Bahjurah, and Farshut, 33–36.

prepared, and the metropolitan was moved there until the repairs were finished. Fr. Pola spent the night with him there.

At approximately 8:30 the following morning, Fr. Luka al-Gawargi came to the retreat house to ask Fr. Pola for something. Fr. Luka entered the room, but it was empty; he did not find Metropolitan Mena on the bed, though he knew he had been moved there the night before.

Fr. Luka asked Fr. Pola, "Where is His Eminence?"

Fr. Pola went into the room and also found it empty. Together, the two monks began to search the rooms of the retreat house, but he was nowhere to be found. The man was unable to walk!

Fr. Luka telephoned an acquaintance in Girga, Mr. Maurice Maqar, and notified him that Metropolitan Mena had gone missing, and urged him to tell no one. A monastery-wide search was quietly prompted for the nearly-disabled metropolitan, in all chapels, cells, and buildings. The search turned up nothing.

There is a neglected indoor garden, under lock and key, behind the retreat house on the monastery grounds. Used as a make-shift storage room, this area was blocked off by a pile of massive wooden logs, among other damaged items, which prevents entry to, or exit from, the room. After about an hour of searching, with no other place left unturned, Fr. Pola decided to unlock this room, for which he alone had the key.

To his surprise, glancing over the pile of wood, he saw Metropolitan Mena sitting comfortably in a chair deep within the garden!

Fr. Pola immediately called several monastery laborers to the garden. While partaking in the considerable group effort to move the heavy logs, Fr. Pola looked up and asked, bewildered, "How did you get in here?"

He immediately yelled out, "This subject is off limits! I'm begging you!"

With the wood finally moved away from the door, Metropolitan Mena could be carried out the exit and brought back to the retreat house.[118]

---

118 Ibid., 15–16.

*Metropolitan Mena with his disciples, Fr. Luka (top)
and Fr. Pola (bottom)*

CHAPTER NINE

His Illness and Sudden Departure

I Found Him and Brought Him Back!

Mr. Malak Anwar Abdel Malak recalls an instance that occurred when Metropolitan Mena's condition began to worsen:

Because of the severity of his ascetic life, his health eventually declined. He developed a hernia, which worsened significantly with age. We brought several well-known physicians to the monastery, and they unanimously agreed that surgery was urgently required.

He underwent the operation, and even while under general anesthesia, the surgeons found that he was praying the psalms, praises from the Midnight Praises, and hymns.

After the surgery, he was placed on a hospital bed fitted with side railings to prevent any movement or risk of falling. Because of the exhaustion of the journey to the hospital, the procedure itself, and the days surrounding it, we all fell into a deep sleep.

At around 3:00 a.m., we were suddenly awakened by a knock on the door of the room. Startled, we got up and were astonished to find His Eminence walking in, supported by a nurse who was holding his arm.

Alarmed by what we saw, we asked him, "What happened, Your Eminence? How did you get out of bed? And how did you leave without us noticing, when we were sleeping right beside you?"

We then turned to the nurse and asked what had occurred. She replied, "I don't know. Suddenly, we found His Eminence on the ground floor, going from room to room, knocking on doors and entering the rooms of the sick. He would pray over them and bless them. He went through the entire floor, then ascended to the floor above and did the same. After that, I found him and brought him back here."

We pleaded with him, saying, "Your Eminence, you have just undergone a serious surgery. Please rest and allow yourself to recover!"

Yet, such instances had become familiar to us through our time with him.[119]

His Blessed Repose

Metropolitan Mena was preparing to travel from the Monastery of the Archangel to Cairo for routine lab tests and a medical follow-up. Aside from a mild chest infection, his health was stable. His recent tests, including blood sugar and liver and kidney functions, were all normal. He remained in

---

119 Video Interview taken from *Al-Zāhid: Suṭūr min Ḥayāt Muthallath Al-Raḥamāt Al-Anbā Mīnā Muṭrān Jirjā* [The Ascetic: Lines from the Life of the Thrice-Blessed Anba Mena, Metropolitan of Girga], on November 6, 2025.

regular contact with his personal physician, Dr. Nabil Saber, who saw no cause for concern before the trip.

Fr. Pola al-Gawargi accompanied him to Cairo. While they were in the car, Metropolitan Mena suddenly turned to Fr. Pola and said calmly, "I am going to repose. Pope Kyrillos and Fr. Abdel Massih will come and take me."

Immediately after saying this, his condition suddenly worsened. Fr. Pola immediately arranged for him to be taken to al-Hayat Hospital in Cairo. Upon arrival, Metropolitan Mena was admitted to the intensive care unit, where he became extremely weak and soon slipped into a semi-coma.

On the morning of Thursday, November 6, 2003, Dr. Nabil Saber arrived at the hospital and was deeply shocked by what he saw. Metropolitan Mena's condition had deteriorated dramatically. This decline was completely unexpected, as his health had been stable before leaving the monastery.

While in the ICU, Metropolitan Mena remained briefly aware at times. He looked around at those near him and tried to lift himself, tightly holding their hands.

"Fr. Abdel Massih…" he whispered, "Pope Kyrillos…"

Dr. Nabil leaned toward him and asked, "Where is Fr. Abdel Massih, Your Eminence? And where is Pope Kyrillos? Are they coming to take you?"

Metropolitan Mena gently nodded. Those present prayed earnestly, hoping for a miracle. But at 3:00 a.m., he fell into a deep coma, and his kidneys stopped functioning.

At 7:30 a.m., Metropolitan Mena stopped breathing. Dr. Nabil immediately began artificial respiration, and the ICU team rushed in to try to revive him. Despite about fifteen minutes of CPR and mechanical ventilation, all efforts were unsuccessful.

At 7:45 a.m., his heart stopped. The appointed time had come for Metropolitan Mena to depart.

On Friday, November 7, 2003, Paope 27, 1720 AM, Metropolitan Mena suddenly and peacefully delivered his soul into the hands of the Lord whom he loved. His eighty-four-year journey on earth had ended. The time came for him to be led into eternity.

Mother Irene, the abbess of the Convent of St. Mercurius in Old Cairo, was receiving treatment at al-Hayat Hospital at the same time. Before his repose, Metropolitan Mena communicated to her that she would be present at his farewell into heaven. She described what she witnessed in a brief account:

On the morning of Friday, November 7, 2003, at 7:45 a.m., I found myself taken [from the hospital] into the midst of a great procession. It accompanied the soul of Abba Mina, Metropolitan of Girga, on its way into Paradise. Leading the procession was the Pure and Holy Virgin Mary. The procession also included the Great Martyr St. Philopater Mercurius, the Great Martyr St. George, Pope Kyrillos VI, and Fr. Abdel Massih of the Monastery of St. Macarius, along with many ranks of heavenly hosts.

When we reached heaven, His Eminence Metropolitan Mina began ascending upward. He advanced toward glory, light, and great splendor.

When he stood before Jesus, the Lord of glory, he bowed down. He worshiped in great humility, and I heard him speak to the Lord of glory, saying, "I am not worthy, my Lord. I am not worthy of all this glory."

Then I heard the voice of the Lord of glory, which was like the sound of thunder, saying to him, "No, Abba Mina. You are worthy. You are worthy because you have fought the good fight, have finished the race, and have kept the faith. You labored and suffered greatly for My sake. Therefore, you are worthy of this glory."

At that moment, I found myself returning and going back to the place where I had been.[120]

*With the late Mother Irene, the abbess of the Convent of
St. Mercurius in Old Cairo*

---

120 A small booklet titled *This is Our Faith: Abba Mena is in Heaven*, page 2, published by the Diocese of Girga, Bahjurah and Farshut on the occasion of his fortieth-day commemoration, and released on Decemeber 18, 2003, records this account, while preserving the anonymity of Mother Irene, since she was still living at the time the account was written.

The funeral procession departed Cairo at exactly 7:00 in the evening. His pure body was brought back to Girga in the early hours of Saturday, November 8. The hearse entered the city at 2:00 a.m., yet it did not arrive at the church of Archangel Michael until 6:00 a.m. The roads were overwhelmed by tens of thousands of mourners who had poured out into the streets, and the procession advanced at a near standstill. Hundreds of security forces were dispatched, and yet they had no power over the crowds. What should have been a brief journey of barely a mile stretched into more than four hours because of the sheer magnitude of love and grief that filled the city.

Even the Muslims, who were fasting during the month of Ramadan at the time, stood among the mourners, as well. And so great was their love for Metropolitan Mena that they did not leave the procession, even to attend their suhoor prayers at the mosque.

Twenty bishops from all across the country traveled to take part in praying the funeral prayers. Following the funeral, Metropolitan Mena was laid to rest in the church of Fr. Abdel Massih, in the tomb prepared beside the sanctuary itself, there to await the resurrection among the saints.

The funeral of the Thrice-Blessed Metropolitan Mena

*Following his burial beside the sanctuary of the
church of Fr. Abdel Massih*

Bibliography

Al-Ashmawy H., *Al-ʾIkhwān Wa-al-Thawrah* [the Brotherhood and the Revolution] 1. (Cairo, Egypt, *Al-Maktab al-Miṣrī Al-Ḥadīth li-Al-Ṭibāʿa Wa-Al-Nashr* [The Modern Egyptian Bureau for Printing and Publishing], 1977).

Athanasius of Alexandria, *The Life of Antony: The Coptic Life and the Greek Life*, Vivian T. and Athanassakis A.N., trans. (Kalamazoo, MI: Cistercian Publications, 2003).

Atiya A.S., ed. "*Abd al-Masih Salib al-Masuʿdi*," in Aziz S. Attiya, ed. *The Coptic Encyclopedia* 1. (New York: Macmillan, 1991), 7b. Online at Claremont Coptic Encyclopedia: https://ccdl.claremont.edu/digital/collection/cce/id/18/rec/16

Atiya, A.S., ed. "*John Sabas*," in Aziz S. Attiya, ed. *The Coptic Encyclopedia* 4. (New York: Macmillan, 1991), 1369a. Online at Claremont Coptic Encyclopedia: https://ccdl.claremont.edu/digital/collection/cce/id/1123/rec/1

Children of Metropolitan Mena, *Al-Anba Mena Al-Sa'eh Wa Al-Aba' Al-Sowah* [Metropolitan Mena the Anchorite and the Anchorite Fathers]. (Girga, Sohag: Diocese of Girga, Bahjurah, and Farshout).

Craton O., *Holy Fools: The Lives of Twenty Fools for Christ.* (Chesterton, Indiana: Ancient Faith Publishing, 2024).

Fanous D., *A Silent Patriarch: Kyrillos VI (1902-1971), Life and Legacy*. (Yonkers, NY: St. Vladimir's Seminary Press, 2019).

Kamal, Hegumen Youannis. *Qiddīsīn Taz̄āharū Bi-Al-Gunūn* [Saints Who Feigned Madness]. (Shubra, Egypt: Dar al-Geel Printing Press, 2006).

Kyrillos M.G., *Al-Qalb Al-Baseer: Ayam Modee'a Fee Hayat Muthalath Al-Rahamat Niyafat Al-Anba Mena Mutran Girga: Hayah - Mungazat - Fada'el – Mo'gizat* [The Discerning Heart: Illuminated Days in the Life of the Thrice-Blessed Metropolitan Mena of Girga: His Life, Achievements, Virtues, and Miracles]. (Girga, Sohag: Diocese of Girga, Bahjurah, and Farshout. 2004).

Metropolitan Mena, *Seerit Qidees Mo'aser: Al-Qis Abd Al-Messih Al-Maqari* [The Life of a Contemporary Saint: Fr. Abd Al-Messih Al-Maqari]. (Al-Manahra, Beni Suef: Committee of Editing and Publication of the Diocese of Beni Suef and Bahnasa, 1979).